CW00747354

finally, helpful sex advice!

finally, helpful sex advice!

A PRACTICAL GUIDE TO SEX

MEG-JOHN BARKER AND JUSTIN HANCOCK

ICON

This edition published in the UK in 2018 by
Icon Books Ltd, Omnibus Business Centre,
39–41 North Road, London N7 9DP
email: info@iconbooks.com
www.iconbooks.com

First published in the UK in 2017 by Icon Books Ltd

Sold in the UK, Europe and Asia
by Faber & Faber Ltd, Bloomsbury House,
74–77 Great Russell Street,
London WC1B 3DA or their agents

Distributed in the UK, Europe and Asia
by Grantham Book Services,
Trent Road, Grantham NG31 7XQ

Distributed in Australia and New Zealand
by Allen & Unwin Pty Ltd,
PO Box 8500, 83 Alexander Street,
Crows Nest, NSW 2065

Distributed in South Africa by
Jonathan Ball, Office B4, The District,
41 Sir Lowry Road, Woodstock 7925

Distributed in India by Penguin Books India,
7th Floor, Infinity Tower – C, DLF Cyber City,
Gurgaon 122002, Haryana

Distributed in Canada by Publishers Group Canada,
76 Stafford Street, Unit 300,
Toronto, Ontario M6J 2S1

Distributed in the USA
by Publishers Group West,
1700 Fourth St., Berkeley, CA, 94710

ISBN: 978-178578-387-6

Text copyright © 2017 Meg-John Barker and Justin Hancock

The authors have asserted their moral rights

No part of this book may be reproduced in any form, or by any
means, without prior permission in writing from the publisher.

Typeset in Adobe Caslon by Marie Doherty

Printed and bound in Great Britain by Clays Ltd, Elcograf S.p.A.

About the Authors

Dr Meg-John Barker is the author of a number of popular books on sex, gender and relationships, including *Queer: A Graphic History* (with Julia Scheele), *How To Understand Your Gender* (with Alex Iantaffi), *Rewriting the Rules*, *The Psychology of Sex* and *The Secrets of Enduring Love* (with Jacqui Gabb). They have also written numerous books, articles, chapters, and reports for scholars and counsellors, drawing on their own research and therapeutic practice. In particular they have focused their academic-activist work on the topics of bisexuality, open non-monogamy, sadomasochism, non-binary gender and Buddhist mindfulness. They blog and podcast about all these topics and more on rewriting-the-rules.com and megjohnandjustin.com. Twitter: @megjohnbarker.

Justin Hancock is a sex and relationships educator, trainer and practitioner working with young people and adults in this field since 1999. His website BISHuk.com is one of the leading sex and relationships advice websites for all those over fourteen and is sponsored by Durex UK. The accompanying book to the website, *Sex Explained: A real and relevant guide to sex, relationships and you*, was self-published in 2013 and was very well received by activists in sex, sexuality and sexual health work such as Brooke Magnanti, Buck Angel and Dr Ranj Singh. In addition to this Justin works with practitioners in sex and relationships education and sexual health services providing training and resources. He was involved in writing teaching resources for the DO SRE for Schools project. He has made a number of media appearances on television and radio and has written several pieces for newspapers and blogs. Twitter: @bishtraining.

Acknowledgements

We'd like to thank Hannah, John, Stephen, Fi, Ben, Petra, Toni and Dean for all their immensely helpful comments on the first draft of the book. We'd also like to thank Kiera from Icon for all her enthusiasm and support with this project, Rhiannon from Hey Kiddo for her invaluable help with our website, and the Open University, Damn Fine Media and Julia Scheele for their input on the additional animations. Thanks also to the people who have taught us so much over the years about sex, too numerous to mention. We're very grateful to the employees and customers at the Barbican and Look Mum No Hands cafes for their patience with two people talking loudly and enthusiastically about sex for hours around a laptop.

Contents

Preface

Hello, and welcome to our sex advice book. Our idea with this book was to give you a practical guide through the confusing, and sometimes daunting, world of sex and sexuality. We wanted to put *your* experience at the heart of the book, and to invite you to explore what might really be enjoyable to you.

For many people even the idea that sex is something we could enjoy is quite radical. In the past, many cultures have tended to be quite *sex negative* – people weren't supposed to enjoy sex but it was more of an obligation or duty linked to having children. These ideas are still very much around, but in recent years a more *sex positive* culture has also come in where we're all supposed to love sex, to be really experimental, and to have incredible orgasms. That can actually put us under just as much pressure and prevent us from really tuning into what we want to do because we're so busy trying to demonstrate how good we are at sex or how much we're enjoying it. We're bombarded by so many messages that we *should* be having sex of a certain kind that we can struggle to even think about what we'd really like to do, let alone communicate that to another person.

In this book we're trying to get away from the sex

negative and sex positive messages to find a kinder way in which we can all approach sex, and enjoy it if we want to.

WHO ARE WE?

A lot of sex advice books claim that the authors are 'sexperts' who can give you 'the secret' to 'great sex'. We're going to challenge all of those ideas over the course of this book! We've learnt a lot about sex over the years, but it's important to remember that only you can be the expert on your experiences, your body and your desires. We're all in this together with the kinds of messages we receive about sex, and we all struggle with them.

This book is the first big project that we've done together after several years of loving each other's work and being great mates. It's the result of many mornings in London cafes sitting together around our laptops with many cups of coffee.

Justin has been a sex educator for a couple of decades, working with young people in schools, youth clubs, and clinics. He also trains other sex educators and runs the BishUK website. Meg-John has studied sex and relationships academically for a similar length of time, as well as working as a sex and relationship therapist, and doing a lot of activism in this area. When we started delivering workshops together and discussing our work we realised that we'd come to similar places from different directions. We noticed similar problems in sex education, sex therapy and sex advice. We hope that by bringing our different knowledge and skills together in this book the result is something new and helpful.

WHO ARE YOU?

When we were writing this book we tried very hard to make sure that it'd be relevant to everyone. A lot of sex advice is written primarily for a certain kind of person in a certain kind of relationship.

We're hoping that the book will particularly appeal to you if you're:

- Somebody who's keen to enjoy sex more than they do

- Somebody who's generally left out of sex advice books (most people!)

- Somebody who hasn't had much sex education, or who's had poor sex education (again, most people!)

- Somebody who isn't doing what they'd really like to do sexually or wants to try different things

- Somebody who's struggling with sex in any way

Obviously we can't cover every single issue that you might have with sex in such a short book. So we've also put together a website (megjohnandjustin.com) where you can ask us your questions, find out more about some of the key ideas in this book, watch animations, and download further resources. We'd also love to hear what you thought of the book over there once you've finished it.

HOW TO USE THIS BOOK

We deliberately started the book with the things that we think are fundamental to enjoying sex: your relationship with yourself and with your body. For this reason it's probably worth going through the book in order, rather than jumping ahead to later chapters. It might seem strange that we don't talk about sex with another person till quite late in the book, but we believe that learning about our own desires, attitudes and feelings about sex is fundamental to being able to communicate about them – and share them – with other people.

We've included lots of activities, things to try, and points for reflection during the book. Hopefully you'll find it useful to pause and have a go at these things. These are the places where you'll probably learn the most about what works for you. We love the idea of people scribbling all over the book, writing in their own ideas and thoughts as they go along. However, we're aware that many of us tend to skip over these parts when we're reading a book like this. That's fine too, you can always bookmark the ones that look useful to you to return to later. The activities are often things we've used in workshops to help people to think more deeply about sex. Most of them can be done by writing things down, talking about them with a friend, or just thinking about them. They'll probably each take between two and ten minutes depending on how much detail you want to go into.

It could be very useful, if you're in a sexual relationship, to do the activities with a partner in order to learn more about each other. However, you might like to do them alone first to get a sense of where you're at without worrying about what they might think of you. There's a lot more about how we talk with partners about sex in Chapter 5. An important point here is that it isn't a good idea to do these activities with anybody who you don't trust, or who is unkind or abusive towards you in any way. If you're unsure whether this applies to you we've included a couple of resources on how to know at the end of the book.

We've also included lots of examples of different people's experiences throughout the book so that you can see the diversity of different things that work for different people. These aren't direct quotes, but they are the kinds of things we've heard several times from people over the years (and some of our own experiences!).

SELF-CARE AND THIS BOOK

Most people find the topic of sex difficult in one way or another. Those who've had sexual experiences may well have had some tough or so-so times along the way. Those who haven't may be worried about what to do, or if they even want to have sex. Also – as we'll see – all of the wider cultural messages about sex can put everyone under a lot of pressure. For that reason it's worth reading this book in a way that's kind to you.

We're going to give a lot of advice about self-care in the next chapter. If that concept is unfamiliar to you it means a similar thing to 'looking after yourself' or 'being kind to yourself'. It's worth thinking about a bit right now in relation to how you read the book. Reading in a self-caring way involves checking out whether you feel in an okay place to do some reading, maybe leaving any sections you know are difficult for you until you're feeling ready for them. You might want to notice your feelings as you go along. If you find yourself feeling a bit uncomfortable reading a certain section that might be a good one to come back to again. Also you can notice when you've read enough for one day and need a bit of time to process it all.

We've tried to write the book kindly as well. We're not aiming to shock anybody or be deliberately provocative. Of course we have had to write about different sexual experiences and practices though. So there is some sexual content, and a few places where we've covered unwanted or non-consensual sexual experiences. In those places we've tried to provide a note up front to let you know that we'll be discussing those topics, and we've never gone into a lot of descriptive detail about those kinds of things.

The introduction will start us thinking more about the messages we all get about sex and how we relate to them. In the next chapter we look more at your particular relationship to sex. Then we have a chapter on bodies and sex, and one on sex in relationships. We end the book with a chapter on communicating consensually about sex, before providing some further resources if you want to carry on the learning you've done here.

Introduction

THE MESSAGES WE RECEIVE ABOUT SEX

Whether we realise it or not, the world around us is saturated with messages about sex. Every day we pick up on loads of ideas about sex from the people around us, from the places we work and play in, and from society more broadly.

Think about the kinds of messages you receive on a daily basis. Perhaps you chat with friends about sex: when it's okay to have sex with a new partner or what counts as 'cheating'. Maybe you pick up magazines with articles about how to have great sex or multiple orgasms, or how to seduce people or be attractive to them. It could be that your religion has ideas about who you're allowed to have sex with and for what purpose. Perhaps you've heard in the news about the latest sexual abuse scandal, or the latest drug for improving 'sexual function'. Probably you'll have seen sexual encounters on TV or in movies that generally follow the same old script. Certainly you'll have seen advertisements on the street or public transport for dating agencies, or for products designed to make you look sexier.

These messages about what sex is (and isn't), how to have it, and who to have it with, tend to be remarkably similar wherever they come from. Because they're all around us they have a major role in shaping how we think and feel about sex, and, therefore, our experience of sex itself.

Because these messages surround us all of the time, most people end up acting on them, and sharing the same ideas when they talk about sex. As a result, these messages often feel like the 'normal' or 'natural' way of doing things, rather than just one possible way of thinking about sex.

Examining these messages – what we learn from them, and whether they're a good fit for us or not – will be a major focus throughout this book. Let's start by thinking about the ideas we receive about what sex actually is.

try it now   WHAT IS SEX (ACCORDING TO THE MESSAGES WE RECEIVE)?

Over the course of this book we'll encourage you to come up with a list of as many sexual, erotic or sensual practices as you can. This kind of list is incredibly helpful for tuning into what you like sexually, and for communicating about that with other people. For now, we'll use it to think more about the sexual messages we receive.

Make a list of all the sexual activities that you can think of – off the top of your head – which people might enjoy. If you have some Post-it notes or small scraps of paper you might like to write one activity on each of these. You're going to be moving them around, so it's useful to have them on separate pieces of paper. If you can't do that where you are right now just jot them down on a piece of paper or think of them. Or you could make a list on your phone or computer and then move them around there.

Allow yourself to think about all of the things that people commonly imagine when it comes to sexual, erotic or sensual experiences. But once you've done that try to think of the less obvious kinds of things as well, like all the different ways you could touch or be touched, or non-touch based things like sharing fantasies. Think of things you'd like yourself and things that you wouldn't particularly like yourself but that maybe other people might like. Try to be quite specific. For example instead of 'oral sex' you might divide it into kissing, licking, sucking, etc. and be clear which part of the body is receiving it.

Now imagine a line like the one below: a spectrum from 'definitely not sex' to 'definitely sex'. Try to arrange your sexual practices along this line, so that the ones that are generally not seen as 'proper sex' go at the left-hand side, the ones that are generally seen as counting as 'proper sex' go at the right-hand side, and any that are somewhere in between go in the appropriate place along the line.

Definitely not sex
Definitely sex

What do you notice about the kinds of things that you put at the far right? What about the far left? Were there any things that you struggled to know where to put? Were there any things that seemed to go in more than one place?

Thinking back to what we were talking about before, do you think that the messages we receive about sex are part of the reason why you've put certain things in certain places?

Keep hold of your list or Post-it notes. We'll be coming back to them in later chapters. Also feel free to keep adding to your list as you go through the rest of the book.

When we've asked groups of people to do this exercise during workshops, they generally come up with this kind of response:

Definitely not sex ←————————————————————→ Definitely sex

Hand-holding | Kisses | Masturbation | Porn | Penis-in-Vagina intercourse
Oral sex
Cuddles | Frotting | Spanking | Anal sex
Massage | Fantasy | Dry humping | Three-some

It seems that things that people count as 'proper sex' generally involve genitals, nudity, and some form of penetration. Often the kinds of sex that involve one penis and one vagina are seen as being somewhat more 'proper' or 'real' than those involving different genitals in different combinations, or other parts of the body. Things at the 'definitely not sex' end of the continuum could be done for other reasons than sexual desire, or are generally seen as potentially *leading to* 'proper sex', rather than *being* sex themselves. Also, activities that don't involve any physical contact often get placed further towards the 'definitely not sex' end of the spectrum.

IS IT HELPFUL TO DIVIDE UP SEX IN THIS WAY?

Can you see any problems with thinking about sex in this way: drawing lines between what counts and what doesn't count as 'proper sex'? You might consider who is able to have 'proper sex' according to this continuum, and who is always going to end up having something less than 'proper sex'. Think about the impact this might have on them and the kinds of pressures it might put on people and their bodies that sex is seen in this way. You might also like to start thinking about how it impacts you specifically. Is there any good reason for saying that some kinds of sex are more 'proper' than others?

Hold onto your thoughts on these issues because we'll be coming back to them towards the end of this chapter.

UNDERSTANDING SEX

If we're able to let go of the ideas about what is 'proper' sex, we may find that we're more able to tune into what we actually enjoy. It's about finding out what works for us rather than trying to match up to an ideal of what we've been told sex is.

try it now ENJOYABLE AND NOT-SO-ENJOYABLE SEX

Think of one kind of sexy, sensual or erotic activity that you've had which you've enjoyed a lot on one occasion, but also not enjoyed as much on another occasion. For example, it might be that you've had a really great kiss one time and – another time – a kiss that left you cold. Or you could pick sex with a partner or on your own, having a fantasy, or something less sexual like a massage. The important thing is that it is the same activity, so that you can compare what it's like when it's enjoyable and when it isn't. For the 'not enjoyable' time, don't pick anything that is scary or upsetting to remember – just a time when you weren't really enjoying it as much as you'd have liked.

Try to remember both experiences – the time when you enjoyed it and the time when you didn't – in rich detail. You could do this as a writing exercise, writing a paragraph or two about each time in turn. Or you could just sit quietly and remember each time in as much detail as possible. You could even create a drawing or cartoon of the experience, with or without words. Either way, you might find the following prompts helpful.

For each experience (the enjoyable one, and the not-so-enjoyable one), think about:

- *How it started:* Where were you? What was happening beforehand? How did it begin? How did you feel? What were the sensations involved? What thoughts were going through your head?

- *How it progressed:* What happened next? What were your feelings, sensations, thoughts? (You might remember some of these more easily than others and that's fine.) Run through the time in your head, continuing to tune into the feelings, sensations and thoughts.

- *How it ended:* What was that like? How did you feel afterwards?

Now think about any differences that you notice between the enjoyable experience and the not-so-enjoyable experience. For example, there might have been differences in the circumstances of the experience: what was happening before and after; who you were doing it with, if anyone; how you felt, or the thoughts that were going through your head. Make a note of anything at all that occurs to you.

MULTIPLE EXPERIENCES: DIFFERENCES BETWEEN ENJOYABLE AND NOT-SO-ENJOYABLE SEX

When we've done this activity before with people, these are the kinds of differences that have come up:

- *How 'in the moment' or 'present' they felt.* For example, people said things like: 'I was less distracted in the enjoyable time, not worrying about what was going to happen next.'

- *Whether they made comparisons between themselves and other people.* For example: 'In the less enjoyable time I kept thinking: "Am I as good as their ex?", "Are they enjoying this as much as last time?", "Do I look as good as people in porn?"'

- *How focused they were on achieving a goal.* For example, in the less enjoyable time people wondered things like: 'Am I going to come?', 'Are they going to come?', 'Am I lasting long enough?' or 'Am I hard/wet/aroused enough?'

- *Whether they were seeing sex as a performance.* For example, in the less enjoyable time people worried: 'Do they think I'm skilled enough at this?' or 'Should I be changing position more?'

- *How consensual it felt.* For example, in the less enjoyable time: 'I felt like I was doing it for them rather than for me,' 'I knew they felt a bit pressured into it' or 'I was a bit part in their scene rather than a central character in my own.'

- *How aware they are of their sensations.* For example: 'When I was enjoying it, I could feel this tingling sensation in my feet, their breath on my skin, the heat rushing to my face. It was like I was totally in my body.'

- *How focused they were on what they thought they should be doing.* For example, in the less enjoyable time people wondered: 'Is it okay to touch them like this? Will they think this is weird? How long should I do this for?'

- *How critical they felt about themself or anyone else involved.* For example, in the less enjoyable time people thought about themselves: 'You look really bad in this position,' 'They're not enjoying this' or 'You're no good at this.' Or they thought about another person: 'Why don't you know what to do?'

'How long is this going on for?' 'You suck – and not in a good way!'

- *How connected they felt with themself or anyone else involved.* For example, in the less enjoyable time: 'I just went with it because I wanted to do it.' Or in the enjoyable time: 'It felt like giving myself a gift,' 'I really felt we were sharing something,' 'It was really intimate' or 'They seemed to really get me.'

Recognising these kinds of differences – between enjoyable and less enjoyable sex – will, over the course of this book, help us to consider how to let go of some of the messages that we receive about sex, how to tune into ourselves and be present, and how to communicate with other people about what we want to do.

FOCUSING ON PROPER SEX OR ENJOYABLE SEX?

If you compare your ideas about enjoyable sex to the previous activity determining what sex *is*, you might well notice that the differences between enjoyable and not-so-enjoyable experiences could apply to pretty much anything on that list, not just the activities that are often seen to count as 'proper sex'. It seems like, when it comes to enjoyable sex, it ain't what you do; it's the way that you do it!

When we focus on distinguishing proper from not proper sex, it's all about which bodies are involved and what they *should* do to each other. When we focus instead on distinguishing enjoyable from less enjoyable sex, the emphasis is much more on how we relate to ourselves and each other, and what we might *like* to do. In other words, it's more about *how* you do things rather than *what* you do. This is not to say – of course – that everybody would (or should) enjoy all of the possible sexual activities if they just did them in the right way. Rather it's about giving us clues about how we can do the things that we prefer in the ways that will be most enjoyable. This book is about figuring out which activities or practices *you* find enjoyable (and less enjoyable) and how you can go about doing them in the most enjoyable ways.

We've deliberately tried to include all sexual experiences equally, rather than buying into the idea that some are 'better', more 'proper' or more 'normal' than others. Whoever you are and whatever you like, you're included in this book. Plus – as we saw in the last activity – the whole idea of 'properness' or 'being normal' seems to interfere with actually enjoying sex. We often stop enjoying sex when we're preoccupied by questions of whether we're doing it properly, how we compare against some ideal or norm, or how we measure up. It's clear that narrow, limited ideas about sex are actually bad for all of us, meaning that we're less likely to enjoy sex, and more likely to have problems with it. Expanding our erotic and sensual imaginations is helpful for everyone.

Beyond penis-in-vagina

One major example of this limited view of sex is the idea that penis-in-vagina (or PIV) sex is the most 'proper' form of sex, and that any other forms of sex are simply 'foreplay' before this 'main act'. Obviously this is a problem because it excludes lots of people, including those who enjoy sex on their own or with someone with the same genitals as themselves. However, it's also a problem for lots of people who could potentially have PIV sex. For example, studies that focus on women generally find that over two thirds of women aren't able to orgasm from just PIV sex, and that most of them need different kinds of sexual activity in order to enjoy sex – such as oral sex, rubbing the clitoris with their hand, or using a vibrator. Also, sex therapists have found that the pressure to get an erection, in order to have PIV sex, can often actually have the opposite effect – the erection gets lost.

A major recent UK survey[1] found that around half of respondents saw themselves as having a sexual difficulty, such as losing erections or not getting orgasms. Perhaps a key reason for this is the emphasis that's placed on having 'normal' as opposed to enjoyable sex, based on quite a limited idea of what counts as normal.

---

[1]   ncbi.nlm.nih.gov/pmc/articles/PMC3898902/

APPROACHING SEX ADVICE

A while ago we were involved in a research project for which we examined popular sex advice in the bestselling sex manuals, sex advice columns, TV documentaries and websites. Of course, all of this sex advice was written by people who want you to have more enjoyable sex. However, we found that the advice most of them offered wasn't very helpful because of the assumptions it made about both sexual 'problems' and how to solve them.

THINK ABOUT IT: SEX ADVICE

Before we go on, think about the other sex advice that you've come across over the years.

- What kinds of sex advice have you engaged with?

- Was it useful to you? In what ways was it useful or not useful?

- What did you want from it? Did you get what you wanted?

- Did you find that it was relevant to you personally? Do you think it would be helpful to everyone?

THE PROBLEM ACCORDING TO SEX ADVICE

In general, sex advice makes the following assumptions about sex:

- People need to have sex, both for their own health and to keep their relationship going.

- Sex is only acceptable in a certain context – generally a committed, monogamous relationship or more 'casual sex', which is aiming towards a monogamous relationship.

- Sex generally means penis-in-vagina (PIV) intercourse, leading to orgasm for one or both people.

This means that the problem which most sex advice addresses is how we can keep having this kind of sex in long-term relationships or, sometimes, how we can get into a long-term sexual relationship in the first place (e.g. through dating or seduction).

For this reason, the solutions that sex advice offers are pretty narrow because they need to ensure that people keep having sex of a certain kind. The most common advice given takes the following forms:

- Vary the positions in which you and your partner have PIV sex, or vary where you do it or what you wear. This is why a lot of sex manuals are mostly given over to illustrations of people having sex in different positions.

- 'Spice up' your sex life by adding other things to the menu, such as sex toys, sharing fantasies, 'mild kink' and different 'foreplay' techniques. Generally, these things are all about making the PIV sex that people have more exciting, and there are often also warnings in this kind of sex advice about not going 'too far' into kink, porn or sex with more than one person.

As you can see, the focus in sex advice tends to be on learning *techniques* for making you 'better' at sex, rather than about tuning into what you want – or don't want – sexually, or how you might communicate about that with others. The idea is that sex is something that you do *to* another person, and that you can improve this, rather than seeing sex as an interaction between you and another person or people, or with yourself. For example, a lot of sex advice tells you how to give a 'perfect blow job', when actually not everybody enjoys getting a blow job, and those who do like lots of different kinds of sensations – they're not all the same.

What we really noticed in most sex advice was how little attention was given to consent. The common view is that there's a set of techniques that everyone will inevitably enjoy: a kind of one-size-fits-all way of having good sex. Therefore, there's no need to get or give consent. For example, sex advice often gives readers examples of 'surprises' that they might like to give their partner – such as tying them up for sex. This is very risky because it doesn't recognise that people are actually very diverse in terms of what they enjoy sexually, if they even enjoy sex at all. What is one person's biggest fantasy will be another person's worst nightmare!

The danger with this kind of sex advice is that it ends up creating the very problems that it's trying to fix. It reinforces narrow ideas about what 'counts' as sex; it puts people under pressure to 'perform' this kind of sex well; and it makes people feel bad if they can't do these things, or don't want to. It also doesn't offer people much in terms of how to ensure that the sex they're having is consensual, which is a real problem when we look at the high proportion of people who have experienced abusive or non-consensual sex – and the toll that that takes.

A DIFFERENT APPROACH TO SEX ADVICE

Let's replace these unhelpful assumptions made by popular sex advice with new, inclusive and flexible beliefs:

- *You can have sex if you want to, but you certainly don't have to have sex.* People differ a lot in terms of sexual desire (from no desire to high desire), and this changes over time as well. Plenty of people, and relationships, are perfectly happy and healthy without any sex.

- *Sex can happen in all kinds of contexts, not just between two partners in a relationship.* For example, sex can include watching porn, fuckbuddy arrangements, threesomes, seeing a sex worker, wanking, orgies, hook-ups, being a sex worker, reading and writing erotic fiction, sex with an ex, etc.

- *There are all kinds of sexual practices, none of which is any better or worse than any other.* Think back to the lists you made earlier. All of these practices will be the most enjoyable kind of sex for somebody somewhere.

Instead of looking for the 'solutions' offered by much mainstream sex advice, think about how you can try out different ideas. We hope this approach will be rather more helpful, and in the chapters to come we'll be looking to turn a number of ways of thinking about sex advice on their head:

- Instead of offering different positions for PIV, we'll expand our erotic and sensual imaginations to encompass the variety of possibilities available, continually questioning the idea of 'normal' or 'proper' sex.

- Instead of suggesting techniques that you could develop, we'll tune into what you enjoy sexually – whatever enjoyment means to you – and how you might be present to sex rather than comparing your experience against some ideal of how sex should be.

Consent lies at the very heart of this book, as it does with enjoyable sex, so we'll always ask how we can maximise the likelihood that we and our partners feel fully able to communicate openly about our desires and turn-offs. This will come with lots of practical advice about how you can actually do this in a world where talking directly about sex is still taboo.

EVERYBODY IS DIFFERENT

Remember that everybody is different. Different things work for different people, and for the same person at different points in their life. For instance, we're diverse in terms of:

- Whether we're sexual at all

- What kinds of things turn us on – if anything

- What kind of bodies we have now, had in the past and may have in the future

- How our bodies work, have worked and will work in the future

- What we like to do physically (or not)

- Why we want to have sex, if we do, and what we get out of it

- The contexts in which we like to have sex or physical intimacy.

As well as being different for different people, all of these things change over time even for the same person. So there really can't be one-size-fits-all sex advice. Rather, sex advice is about learning a set of ideas and tools that will continue to be helpful to us over the course of our lives.

This different approach to sex isn't simple or easy – it's going to take some work. A lot of the messages that we receive about sex are deeply ingrained – to the extent that many sex advisors don't even really question them.

Trying a different approach involves stepping outside of what is considered 'normal', and that's often a tough thing to do. For example, how easy is it to think of solo sex as just as valuable as sex with a partner? Or to be comfortable with sex that doesn't involve any kind of penetration? Even as sex advisors, we often find that we fall back into criticising ourselves or worrying about whether we're having 'proper' sex, and we've been thinking about these ideas for a long time!

WE ALL NEED TO REMEMBER

- It's very hard to step outside of popular ideas and assumptions about sex; so go easy on yourself as you think about these things.

- This isn't about replacing one set of rules about sex with another set. Rather, it's about really tuning into yourself and to how you want to do things.

- It's important to treat yourself kindly and to take this at your own speed. As we'll see, it can take a while to really be present to yourself and to find a different way of relating to sex.

You and Sex

The last chapter covered the kinds of messages that we all receive about sex from the world around us, explaining how difficult it can make sex because of the assumptions and expectations that we have. We explained that this is why we need to be very kind and gentle with ourselves: because we're under a lot of pressure about sex, and it's hard to find ways to approach it differently.

Now we're going to get more personal. While we all receive similar messages about sex, the specific messages that you received growing up, and the impact they've had on you, will be unique. Similarly, while it's important that we all look after ourselves and treat ourselves gently when it comes to sex, the ways of doing this that work best will be different for each of us.

So, this chapter begins by helping you explore your own relationship to sex in more detail. Then we'll consider how you can do some self-care in relation to these areas and how to be present to sex – rather than coming at it with a load of expectations – and how you can tune into your own sexual desires.

Hopefully you can see why it's important to start with your relationship with yourself: if you haven't thought about your ideas concerning sex, or how you feel about yourself, it can be quite difficult to tune into what you want and to communicate about this with other people.

YOUR MESSAGES, BACKGROUND AND EXPERIENCES

A lot of sex advice focuses on biological and physiological aspects of sex. Think about the search for the 'female Viagra', the fixation on a position that will stimulate the 'g-spot', or the assumption that it's important for men to 'last longer' or 'stay hard'.

This kind of advice risks ignoring, or skating over, the psychological and social aspects of our lives. These are at least as important as the biological aspects in making up our sexual experience. That's why we like to use the word '*biopsychosocial*' when talking about sexual experiences.

Obviously, how our particular body works is important, but equally important are the kinds of messages that we receive about sex, and how we personally feel about sex. For example, if a person finds it painful to be penetrated, lack of lubrication might be part of the picture, but at least as important could be the fact that they feel they should have a certain kind of sex in order to keep their relationship, and the anxiety they have about that.

Another problem with biologically focused advice is that it often assumes that everybody is the same, so it offers a one-size-fits-all solution. The idea is that if it works for the writer then it'll work for the reader, because we all have the same kinds of bodies, genitals and hormones – right? We don't think so. We assume that your experiences will be different in all kinds of ways to our own.

First, it isn't true that all bodies are the same. Also, if we recognise the importance of psychological and social aspects, then we really begin to see how everybody's experience of sex is different. The way that the biological ('bio'), the psychological ('psycho') and the social combine is unique for each person given the differences between us in our identities, our communities, the ways we were brought up, the sexual experiences we've had, what turns us on, and so on.

So, the word 'biopsychosocial' indicates that all of those different elements influence each other. The ways in which our bodies and brains work influence psychological things like our sexual desire and how we experience sex. However, our sexual experiences in turn also affect our bodies and brains. For example, when we begin finding a new thing sexually exciting, or get turned off by a bad experience, our bodies and brains may start responding very differently to that stimulus than before. Also, the social world influences all of those things because it's where we find out about what might, or might not, be sexy. And personal sexual experiences eventually influence the social world too, as with increasing acceptance of people with same-sex attraction, for example.

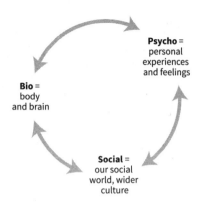

MULTIPLE EXPERIENCES

Here are a few examples of ways in which sex can be biopsychosocial.

- Joe wanted to have sex with his partner but felt ashamed because he couldn't always get an erection. The *biological* part of his experience was his not getting an erection, but this was intrinsically linked with the *psychological* part (he didn't want his partner to think that he didn't fancy them) and the *social* part (the messages they'd both received that men are supposed to get hard when they're attracted to someone, and that in order to have sex you have to have a hard-on).

- Kat remembers a time when she was a kid and saw a James Bond movie where Bond was tied to a chair by the bad guy. Something about this excited her, and she often used to think about it on her own at night. As time passed this became part of her sexual fantasies. She eventually found other people who were into bondage, and it became a great part of her sex life. In this case a *social* thing (the movie) influenced the *psychological* (her fantasies) and the *biological* (the way parts of her body and brain connected).

- Ali was very frustrated because they really wanted to have sex with their new partner Jay. In fact, they wanted to 'get fucked hard' by them! Ali got the impression that Jay was being cautious because of Ali being disabled. In this case the physical (*bio*) aspects of Ali's body were interwoven with strong *social* assumptions (about disabled people not being sexual), and this affected the *psychological* relationship between Ali and Jay, and their sexual experiences.

You might want to pause now and take some time to think about some of the key biological, psychological and social aspects of your own experiences, and how they link together. Can you see how unique this makes you and your sexuality? And how unique it makes all of us in terms of how our bodies work, what turns us on, or what we're looking for?

YOUR BACKGROUND

Let's think a bit about your own background in relation to sex. This should help you to get more of a sense of how you've ended up where you are now in terms of the ideas that you have about sex, how you feel about it, what you like and dislike, and so on.

As you go through this section, don't worry about what you come up with. There are no rights or wrongs here. People learn about sex in all kinds of different ways, and at different times. You might have lots of memories about these things, none at all, or anything in between, and that's fine. The idea here is that uncovering what we've learnt about sex can help us to unlearn unhelpful ideas, and instead learn more helpful ways of thinking about sex.

THINK ABOUT IT: WHAT YOU LEARNT ABOUT SEX

Think about what you learnt about sex through your childhood and adolescence. Remember that sometimes the things we learn are the things that *aren't* said rather than the things that *are* (for example, when a teacher shut down a conversation, or a parent looked embarrassed when something came on TV, or the things that weren't covered in sex ed). Think about:

- Things that were said directly to you about what was and wasn't okay to do, for example, in your family

- Sex education that you received at school or in your community

---

- The language that was used around sex

- What you and your friends used to talk about in relation to sex

- What you saw on TV or in other media that related to sex

- The guesses that you made about sex before you had much information

You might like to write down, or think of, a list of the main things that you learnt about sex growing up. It's okay if things don't immediately spring to mind: it often takes a while to get used to thinking back to our early messages. If you can think of something, you might like to reflect on how these ideas look to you now. Which do you think were valuable, and which less so? Which ones did you hear from lots of places and which ones were just one-offs that stuck with you? What would you add to the list now, as an adult? What would you remove from it?

We all carry around with us a lot of what we learnt about sex from a young age. Many of these things have been reinforced by the messages around us, and we've acted on them many times as well, so they often feel very 'normal' or 'natural'. Actually, it's important to remember that they are only what we've learnt, and they could be otherwise.

For example, a lot of people find it really difficult to talk about sex. They might assume it's just normal and natural to find talking about sex awkward. However, if they think about what they learnt growing up, they might remember how embarrassed and inhibited their parents and teachers were about sex, and how they were told off when they brought up the subject in public. So, this isn't the *only* way to think about sex, it's just what a lot of us learn, and it could be otherwise.

It's important to remember, of course, that the process of re-learning these kinds of things isn't easy. But if we come from a place of understanding about the things we've learnt in the past, then we have a better idea of what this process might involve.

FIRST SEXUAL EXPERIENCES

As well as thinking about the messages we've received and internalised about sex, it can be useful to reflect on our early sexual experiences. These are a major part of what creates our template for what sex is, what turns us on, and how we relate to our bodies.

We could divide early sexual experiences into the following four elements: fantasies, self-touch, unwanted experiences with others, and wanted experiences with others. It's through these kinds of experiences that we receive many cultural messages about sex, as well as learning what we ourselves like and don't like. The way these early experiences play out can leave us feeling valued and affirmed, or vulnerable and ashamed, or a mixture of both, and these reactions will influence what we do in future and how we feel about it.

Some people will have experienced all of these four elements, some none, and everything in between. Think about your own early experiences of each of the four.

It's worth noting here that we live in a very non-consensual culture where few of us reach adulthood without some kind of non-consensual sexual experience. Whether that's somebody showing us porn on their phone that we didn't want to see, or being flashed at in the park, other kids making sexual comments as we walk past, being groped at a party, being sent online links to sexual content, or receiving unwanted attention on public transport. For many people, non-consensual experiences have been such an everyday part of their lives that they might not even see them that way. For many women, such experiences can become so commonplace that they may not question them or report them. For many men, the assumption they should enjoy anything sexual means that they may not interpret such experiences as a problem – even when they are.

Because of this, the following examples might be challenging, as they include unwanted early sexual experiences. If you feel like it might be too tough for you to think about these things at the moment, feel free to flip straight onto the next section on page 30: Self-care.

- *Fantasies:* This includes stories you told yourself, dreams and daydreams, images in your mind, and thoughts and imaginings which may or may not have been based on things you have seen, read or heard about. For example: 'I remember seeing a naked woman in a newspaper and imagining being with her on a tropical beach.' 'I remember telling myself exciting stories when I went to bed about naughty children getting punished.'

- *Self-touch:* This includes any kind of touching your own body, which you may or may not have labelled as sexual at the time. For example: 'I remember touching my genital area after going to bed to stop myself needing to go to the loo and realising that it felt good.' 'I remember snuggling up to my mum's satin dress and finding it soothing.' 'I can't remember any kind of self-touch until I was an adolescent and discovered wanking.'

- *Unwanted experiences with others:* This includes anyone saying or doing something sexual that you didn't want. For example: 'I remember a kid flashing his dick at me in the swimming pool and being shocked at how big it was.' 'My uncle used to touch me in a way I found very uncomfortable. It was only later that I realised that it was sexual abuse.' 'Somebody showed me their phone and it was a porn video. I felt turned on by it and confused by that.' 'I was raped by my second boyfriend when I was in my teens.'

- *Wanted experiences with others:* This includes people saying or doing things that you did want. For example: 'I snogged Kimberly Unwin at the bus stop and touched her boob; it was really exciting.' 'I went back with my boyfriend to his college halls, and I knew we were going to have sex for the first time. It felt right but I was also anxious. The first time was okay, but later we woke up and did it again, and that was way better because I was more relaxed.' 'I remember doing "you show me yours and I'll show you mine" in the playground and loving that tickly, thrilling, funny feeling that I got from it.'

What experiences do you recall of each of these four elements? In thinking about this, you may find that you took on messages about sex from quite a young age. It's important to remember that as we go forward. We're unpacking stuff here that we've often learnt from year zero; so go easy on yourself if you're trying to unlearn some of these messages: it will take time. Also, if some of these early experiences had painful or difficult feelings attached – as unwanted and shaming experiences often do – it can take a long time to deal with them. We've included some further resources at the end of the book if this is something you're struggling with.

BECOMING SEXUAL

You might find it useful to revisit the question 'What is sex?' (from page 2) in relation to the four elements of sexual experience activity. Often, our early experiences aren't things that we thought of as sexual at the time. At what point do we start to see them in this way? Are we still not sure whether some of these things were sexual or not? How important is it to draw clear lines between what is and isn't sex?

Sometimes we find that the things we enjoyed when we were younger are seen as 'not proper sex' by other people, or by wider society, and that can make them difficult to incorporate into our sex lives now, even though we might really enjoy them. You might like to think for now about how your early experiences influenced the scripts that you have for sex today – the ways in which you have solo sex, or sex with others, if you do these things.

SELF-CARE

Few of us get through our early lives without learning several messages about sex which leave us feeling self-critical. As we've seen, for example, it might be that we were humiliated for touching ourselves; or perhaps we had unwanted sexual experiences which left us with shame, fear or guilt about sex; or maybe we found that the things that turned us on didn't map onto the 'proper sex' we were learning about.

We live in a world where we're actively encouraged to be self-critical, particularly in the area of sex. Our economy is based on people selling us products, and often they do this by trying to prove that we are lacking in some way, in order that we buy into the idea they are selling, as well as the product itself. Often this focuses on things like our bodies and physical attractiveness, whether we are 'normal' enough, and our relationships with other people. So, we have adverts for beauty products, fashion magazines, self-help books and online dating services which give us direct messages that we might not be attractive enough, normal enough or in a good enough relationship. And we also have subtler messages from Hollywood movies, reality TV shows and other forms of media which present 'perfect' bodies, people and relationships for us to aspire to.

The experiences that we have growing up, and as adults, happen within this cultural context. So, it's very easy for other people to criticise us – and for us to criticise ourselves – in these kinds of ways. We hear our mates joking about how somebody on TV looks, and we start to worry that they think the same things about us. Our parents tell us that we need to toughen up, or look pretty, if we're ever going to get a partner. We think to ourselves that nobody will ever want to have sex with us unless we do the things 'everybody else' does, or look like the ideal 'sexy' bodies in magazines.

For these reasons it is really important that we cultivate self-care, or being kind to ourselves. When we're surrounded by these kinds of messages it takes some effort to counterbalance them and to reach a place where we can be more okay with who we are, how we look and what we might want sexually. When we repeat those self-criticisms over and over again, they become etched onto our bodies and brains, and it's important to start to sketch out a different pattern.

During the rest of this book we're going to talk a lot about how to tune into what you want sexually and how to communicate about it with others. Both of these things need a foundation in self-care. If we're not kind to ourselves, then it's hard to be open to everything we might like sexually because we're so busy judging whether we think it is normal or acceptable enough. We're unlikely to feel comfortable enough to communicate openly with others if we feel a lot of shame, guilt or anxiety about what we enjoy or really want to do. It's also good to give ourselves, and other people, the message that we deserve to be treated kindly.

BUILDING IN SELF-CARE AT MULTIPLE LEVELS

We receive self-critical messages on a number of levels: from wider society; from within our own communities and workplaces; in our relationships with friends, families and partners; and in our own thoughts and feelings.

Each of these levels is embedded within the others, as you can see in the following diagram. For example, imagine someone who has just started college and has the self-critical thought that they're not very good at getting sex. This could well be embedded in conversations with new friends who seem to be finding it so much easier to meet people for sex. It might also be embedded within the new community they find themselves in at college, where there's pressure to hook up with people and to have a reputation as 'up for it' or 'one of the lads', and where condoms are given away to new students, building the expectation that they will all be having sex. The self-critical thought is also embedded in wider culture – for example, in all the newspaper articles that come out every year about student sexual exploits and sex on campus.

You might find it helpful to think of a self-critical thought that you have about sex or relationships and to consider how it is embedded in all these levels in a similar way.

It's very hard to escape self-criticism, given how embedded it is in all our relationships and communities. However, we can start to counter these messages by deliberately building in the *opposite* of criticism on each level. This is where self-care comes in. It's about replacing criticism with kindness whenever we spot it – and also about being kind to ourselves when we don't spot it, or don't manage to replace it, because it's not easy!

Self-help books often give the message that self-care is simple: if we just do something nice for ourselves, then we'll be able to love ourselves and have sex more easily. Actually, it's much more challenging than this. We're often talking about changing the self-critical habits of a lifetime, and even if we change our own habits, we're still embedded in those other levels of criticism. No amount of long, hot baths are going to overcome the strong messages we're receiving every day that we're not okay as we are!

Going back to our student example, let's think about how they could combat self-criticism with self-care on each of the levels they're embedded in.

Individual experience

Starting with their individual experience of self-critical thoughts and feelings, they could try reflecting on what it is they want to get out of sex versus how much they want to do it because that's what's expected. Our student could also try meditation practices for staying with uncomfortable feelings so that this kind of reflection becomes easier. They might try having more solo sex if they're feeling like they want to have sex but not necessarily sex with someone else.

Interpersonal relationships

On the interpersonal level, they could think about how they're seeing the people around them. We often compare our insides to other people's outsides: assuming that everyone else is finding things easier just because they give off that impression. Actually, take it from us, everyone else is just as much of a seething turmoil of self-criticism! Our student could also think about who to talk to, e.g. people from back home, or one or two people they connect with at college. It's possible that a few deeper friendships would enable some more honest conversations about sex. They could think about *how* they communicate. For example, people might be more honest in online communication than in person, or more so in a one-to-one chat than in a group of people. They could consider online forums, texting old friends or going for a coffee with somebody.

Community and institutions

On the community level, our student could think about the groups of people they're mostly engaging with. Not everybody who starts college is trying to have as much sex as possible! For example, there are plenty of societies focused on other things with which they could get involved. It could be possible for our student to point out the problems with the message conveyed in giving free condoms to every student (whether they want them or not, with no further discussion). They could send an email to the student union suggesting a different approach. Closer to home, they could think about the groups they're hanging around with most and whether these match their personality well or not. People generally take some time to settle down in a group of friends at college; you don't have to stick with the people living closest to you, or the first people you meet.

Wider society and cultural messages

Finally, on the wider cultural level, our student could start by recognising the link between social norms and media messages and the way that they are feeling. That might take the weight off our student from feeling that it's them who is somehow 'wrong' or flawed. If they want to engage further, perhaps they could write an alternative perspective for the student newspaper or get involved with projects that are going on – such as groups training people about consent, or Nightline services that support other students who are struggling with these kinds of pressures.

Try going through these levels in a similar way with your own example of a self-critical thought from earlier. How might you build in self-care on each level?

DIFFERENT KINDS OF SELF-CARE

As well as thinking about self-care on different levels, it's also worth considering different kinds of self-care. We don't always need the same thing. For example, when you're feeling totally wrung out and exhausted, you probably just need to do something kind and relaxing. When you're struggling with difficult emotions, it can be good to find a way to listen to them which makes the emotions less overwhelming. And when you're struggling to decide what to do, it can be good to take some time out for reflection.

We could think of these different kinds of self-care as *self-kindness*, *staying with feelings* and *reflection*. It's worth building in some time for all three of these.

MULTIPLE EXPERIENCES

Self-kindness

- 'Once a week or so I have an evening to myself where I make popcorn just the way I like it and watch one of my favourite movies.'

- 'Someone told me that I should have a hot bubble bath surrounded by candles but I hated it! I just felt really hot and needed a shower afterwards to wash off all the gunk. In the end I stopped doing that but started going for a walk in the morning, which works much better for me.'

Staying with feelings

- 'I read this thing about how often it isn't the feelings that are hard, but the feelings we have about the feelings! So now when I'm feeling scared or sad or angry, I try to just stay with that instead of getting into a whole tangle of feelings about how I shouldn't be feeling that way.'

- 'I try to notice my feelings and allow them to happen instead of what I used to do – distracting myself by watching TV or whatever. I try to let them happen, maybe write them down or just sit outside somewhere.'

Reflection

- 'I have one friend who I can talk to about everything. Whenever we get together we do a kind of bullet point list of whatever's going on for both of us at the start of the conversation and then we just cover it all!'

- 'It really helps me to keep a journal where I write out all my thoughts about whatever's going on. At first I really struggled to actually do this, so now I go to my favourite cafe once a week and make it part of a ritual with coffee and cake, so it's a really pleasant experience.'

You can see from these examples that different things work for different people, and at different times. In this way, self-care is just like sex. You need to start by tuning into what you need on this particular occasion, and then find a way of building that in. Sometimes it might be a matter of trying one thing, realising it's not working for you this time, and then trying something else.

try it now DOING SOME SELF-CARE

Think of one example each of self-kindness, of staying with feelings, and of reflection that appeal to you – maybe the examples we've included here or something else. Try to make time over the next fortnight to try each of these things. At the end of that time, think about what worked – or didn't work – for you about each of them.

One way of doing self-care which is very relevant to sex is being present. This can be a form of self-kindness as well as a good practice for staying with feelings.

BEING PRESENT

Remember the activity we did in Chapter 1 about enjoyable versus not enjoyable sex? A common theme of enjoyable sex is that many people feel more 'present': more able to just be in the moment and go with the flow. Maybe you noticed this when you did the activity?

The idea of 'being present' is a key one in the popular approach of mindfulness. It is all about cultivating the capacity to gently be with our experiences as they are, rather than judging them, trying to change them, or looking ahead to what we're doing next. So, for example, if we were doing the washing up, we'd try to just focus on that, feeling the sensations of the hot water, smelling the washing up liquid, experiencing the pleasure of a dish going from dirty to clean. If we found our thoughts wandering off, we'd try to bring ourselves back gently to the experience of washing up.[2]

Being present is also an important part of self-care. It can be a way of treating ourselves kindly. For example, you might go for a short walk and really let yourself notice the sights, sounds and sensations along the way. It can also be a way of learning to stay with feelings, for example, learning forms of meditation where you notice the feelings but don't try to get rid of them or act on them: you just notice their texture and colour, and how they feel in your body.

You could argue that pretty much every other message we've ever received in life has taught us the exact opposite of being present! We're encouraged to be

<hr>

[2]   If you want to know more about mindfulness, or the Buddhist philosophy that it comes from, check out *Mindfulness: Your step-by-step guide to a happier life* (Icon, 2016) and *Introducing Buddha* (Icon, 2008).

constantly striving to meet our goals, to do a bunch of different things all at once, and to always be planning for the future or mulling over the past. We're also told that some emotions are 'negative' and that we should try to get rid of them rather than welcoming them and treating them kindly. For this reason, being present is by no means easy. In fact, lots of Buddhist teachers would tell you that it's a life-long project and that we never completely learn how to be present in every situation.

HOW TO BE PRESENT DURING EVERYDAY LIFE

For some people it can be easier to try cultivating the ability to be present in their everyday lives first, rather than bringing it straight into their sex lives. Many community centres and organisations now have eight-week mindfulness courses that you can take to learn different techniques. Or you could just try making a little time every day for being present, whether that's something formal like sitting and trying to be aware of your breathing going in and out, or something informal like making time to be present to your cup of coffee or tea in the morning. When we're being present to a cup of coffee, we're really paying attention to the aromatic smell, to the sensation of heat in our mouths, to the complex array of tastes as the liquid flows over our tongues, to the feeling of it going down our throats and warming our bodies, and to the sense of alertness that pervades us (if the coffee is caffeinated!) – perhaps a waking up behind the eyes and a general sense of being livelier. Like other forms of self-care, it's all about finding what works for you, because if you don't find it enjoyable at least some of the time you'll struggle to stick with it.

try it now FIVE MINUTES BEING PRESENT

Give yourself five minutes to keep bringing yourself back to the moment, whether that is just sitting and observing your breath or the sounds around you, or doing something like having a drink or going for a short walk. Notice how you get distracted, and gently bring yourself back to your focus when that happens.

HOW TO BE PRESENT DURING SEX

We've seen that many of us are even more self-critical when it comes to sex than we are in other areas, so sex can be the most challenging place to practise being present. We often have all of these self-critical thoughts going around our heads, as well as a strong sense of what we 'should' or 'shouldn't' be doing during sex, and a goal that we are aiming for. Trying to reach a goal (such as an erection, an orgasm or a partner's pleasure) is the complete opposite to being present because we're striving for a destination rather than appreciating the journey.

Being present is probably the key to having enjoyable sex, but everything we're taught about sex is pretty much the opposite of being present – right?

So, how can we actually practise being present during sex? One way is to try to transfer this way of being from non-sexual experiences (such as being present to your cup of coffee) into a sexual context. Imagine being present to a long kiss. You might start by paying closer attention to another person's face, to their eyes as they connect with yours and to the sensation of their breath on your skin. As your lips meet you might notice the softness of the initial connection, maybe the sounds in your body and between you, or a sense of vibration as your bodies get closer. As the lips part you can experience the taste and texture of the inside of their mouth. You might also have sensations in other parts of your body: a tingling on the back of the neck or your hands and feet, a warmth as your bodies get closer. You could also tune into the sense of connection of knowing when to push forward or pull back a little, and how it feels once the kiss is over.

The way we often relate to kissing is very similar to the way we generally relate to coffee. A cup of coffee is frequently something we have quickly at the start of the day to wake us up. We often drink it down quickly to get the effect and fail to notice any of the complex and subtle smells, tastes or sensations that it produces. Similarly a kiss is often seen as a prelude to something else, not something to be enjoyed for its own sake. Slowing down and being present is a way of making every little part of sex into a main event in its own right, not just a thing we do on the way to something else.

You might find it useful to make time for specific sexual, erotic or sensual activities in this way, where you deliberately focus in on them without any pressure for them to lead anywhere at all. This isn't just a way of practising being present, it's also a way of challenging that whole idea of 'proper sex' that we've been talking about: making each activity as valuable as any other.

You might even find that practising being present during sex helps you to do it more in the rest of your life. The more you practise it in one context, the easier it becomes in other contexts.

The main thing that gets in the way of being present are all of the thoughts and feelings that bubble up. These can be anything from the kind of self-criticisms we've explored to more mundane things like wondering if we turned the oven off, or feeling a crick in our neck. When this happens, it's easy to be critical of ourselves for it, which can lead us into a spiral of criticisms about criticisms about criticisms!

For this reason, it's vital to be gentle with ourselves and to recognise that it's inevitable that we will drift off in these kinds of ways. The idea isn't to avoid distraction, but rather to notice when it happens: it is just one more part of our experience to be present to. We can try to bring ourselves gently back to the moment. Often it's useful to return to something like our breath, the sensations in our bodies, or the sounds we can hear. However, if that doesn't come easily, that's fine: it's just one more thing to notice!

A big part of the Buddhist philosophy behind this idea of being present is that we generally spend our lives trying to grasp hold of all the things we want and to get rid of all the things we don't want. Meditation teacher Martine Batchelor gives a really helpful metaphor for this:

> *Let's imagine that I am holding an object made of gold. It is so precious, and it is mine – I feel I must hold onto it. I grasp it, curling my fingers so as not to drop it, so that nobody can take it away from me. What happens after a while? Not only do my hand and arm get cramp, but I cannot use my hand for anything else. When you grip something, you create tension and limit yourself.*
>
> *Dropping the golden object is not the solution. Non-attachment means learning to relax, to uncurl the fingers and gently open the hand. When my hand is wide open and there is no tension, the precious object can rest lightly on my palm. I can still value the object and take care of it; I can put it down and pick it up; I can use my hand for doing something else.*[3]

---

[3] Batchelor, S. & Batchelor, M. (2001). *Meditation for Life.* Somerville, MA: Wisdom Publications.

When it comes to sex we do this all the time. For example, we have lots of ideas about 'successful' sex that we're trying to make happen, and 'unsuccessful' sex that we're trying to avoid. We might think to ourselves 'I must get an erection' and 'it must last more than five minutes,' 'They must get an orgasm,' 'I mustn't let them see my muffin tops,' 'I mustn't fart' or 'I mustn't look ridiculous when I come.' With being present, you're trying to hold sex more lightly and to be with whatever happens, rather than labelling some things 'good' and some things 'bad' like this.

It can be easier to start practising being present during solo sex, fantasies or self-touch because there isn't anybody else present. So, while there may still be self-critical messages around (particularly around whether solo sex is 'proper' sex), there might be fewer concerns – at least about how another person is seeing you.

SELF-TOUCH AND SOLO SEX, FANTASIES, EROTICA AND PORN

A lot of sex advisors cover solo sex, but generally only as a way of 'practising' for the 'real thing'. For example, they suggest that people engage in self-touch to figure out how they like being touched, or to learn how to 'last longer' during sex with another person.

It's important to let go of this idea of what is 'proper' and to focus instead on what you find is enjoyable. Part of that is seeing solo activities as just as legitimate as activities with another person. It's relevant to how we relate to our bodies, and to how we communicate with ourselves and other people about sex, so we'll keep talking about solo sex in all the remaining chapters of this book.

Solo sex covers a very broad range of activities and ideas. As with sex in general, it's not always clear where something starts or stops being sexual. For example, where does self-touch become solo sex? Where does a daydream become a sexual fantasy? The answers will be different for different people.

Obviously it's vital only to do things that are enjoyable to you. Standard sex advice sometimes tells people that they *should* masturbate, often in certain ways, in order to get better at 'proper sex'. Here we'll introduce a wide range of the sexual, sensual and erotic things that you can do alone, but it's totally up to you whether you try any of them or not.

SELF-TOUCH AND SOLO SEX

There's a lot of shame for many people around solo sex and self-touch. We've used both terms here because for some people, touching themselves is a kind of sex, and for others it wouldn't fall into that category. Some people use 'masturbation', 'wanking' or other words for the same experiences.

We're still not that far away from the times when

people bought anti-masturbation devices for their kids and thought that solo sex resulted in all kinds of physical and psychological problems (and in some communities this way of thinking is sadly still the case). Many people still have early experiences of being told off by parents or teachers for touching themselves. There's also a common assumption that masturbating is somehow a 'sad' or 'lonely' activity, and that people in relationships shouldn't need to do it because they should have all of their sexual desires met by a partner.

If you haven't already done so, just reflect for a moment about the cultural messages you've heard about solo sex, and your own early experiences with it, if you have any. Also think about how you – and the people around you in your life – view it now.

For these reasons, people can keep solo sex very private: both the fact that they do it, and what they actually do. Of course this only reinforces that sense of shame about it. No wonder we often feel confused about solo sex when one set of messages is telling us that we *must* do it – to improve our sex lives – and another set of messages is telling us that we *mustn't* do it – because it isn't 'proper' sex and will ruin our sex lives (particularly if it involves watching porn).

Despite this, of course, most people do have solo sex occasionally or regularly. It would be great if we could lift some of the secrecy and shame around it so that people could enjoy it, instead of regarding it as a thing that 'dirty people' or 'losers' do, or as a source of humour and ridicule.

So, let's think a bit about what solo sex actually involves. Media representations of solo sex present a very limited, and gendered, picture, which is very different from the reality of people's lives. For women, solo sex is often seen as a luxurious and self-indulgent thing that they make time for, perhaps surrounded by scented candles! We often see very little of what they actually do, just an image of a woman in a bath, or a joke about 'the rabbit', for example. For men, solo sex is often depicted as wanking, something they have to do in a quick and perfunctory way in response to an uncontrollable urge (seeing an attractive woman, for example).

Solo sex is much more varied than this, and the way people do it isn't tied to gender. It can be anything from a quick orgasm to an evening of fun. Physically it works in very different ways for different people, and it can also be done for widely diverse reasons.

DIVERSE FORMS OF GENITAL SELF-TOUCH

Focusing on the physical, there are of course forms of self-touch that are about enjoying the sensation for its own sake, and there are forms that are aimed towards an orgasm or another form of climax. One obvious example of self-touch is a person touching their own genitals, but there is still massive diversity in the types of touch that work for different people. For example, some people need wetness, whereas others need dry friction, and any kind of lubrication wouldn't work for them at all. Some use hands, others rub against something else like a pillow, or use the water flowing out of a tap or shower, or just squeeze their thighs together. Some need a sensation of suction. For some it's about gentle stroking; others need a really firm grasp or contact.

Some people like to use vibrators, but people are massively varied in relation to whether they want stimulation on one very specific point or over a wider area, and whether they like a soft buzz or a heavy thud, or anything in between. People do it in all different positions: on their backs, sides or fronts, curled up or stretched out.

Some people prefer penetration or insertion instead of, or as well as, external stimulation. Others would hate that. Others differ on different occasions. Insertion is massively varied, and all of the above points apply too in terms of the different kinds of stimulation somebody might want: gentle or firm, rough or smooth, large or small, wet or dry, and so on.

MULTIPLE EXPERIENCES: SELF-TOUCH

Of course, this variety of preferences for solo sex applies across all kinds of self-touch. We'd take up a whole chapter – if not a whole book – to list them all! The following examples are not exhaustive but should give you a sense of the variety of things that people do:

- 'I've always liked the sensation of rubbing my duvet softly against my face. I find it soothing, and there's also something exciting about it.'

- 'I pull my own hair sometimes. There's a frisson sometimes because for me it's a sexual thing, but other people might not be aware of that.'

- 'When I'm alone and turned on, I like to touch parts of my body that I'm not so comfortable with around another person; it helps me feel kinder towards those body parts because I'm focusing on the good feeling rather than how I think they look.'

- 'I stimulate my breasts and nipples, and often that in itself brings me to orgasm.'

- 'I like to lie across the bed as if I were being spanked; sometimes I spank myself a bit. That really turns me on.'

The important thing to do – if you want to – is to experiment with what works for you, rather than limiting yourself to what you might think of as the 'proper' way to do it.

Some people find that they have one very set way of doing self-touch, because they've found something that works for them and have done it over and over. It's great to know how you work in this way, and you might also find it useful and interesting to try other things as well. It can help in terms of exploring what turns you on, and how your body works, to sometimes go outside of your regular habit.

WHY SELF-TOUCH?

Reasons for solo sex and self-touch are just as diverse as the things that people do. For example, reasons people give include: wanting a quick release, to see how something feels (e.g. insertion), feeling really turned on, feeling bored, to reduce anxiety, as a treat, to help them fall asleep, to experiment with a new toy or form of self-touch, to perk them up, to release – or snap out of – a difficult emotional state, as a form of self-care, as a reward for having done two hours of work or similar, to avoid work with a 'procrastibate' (wanking-from-home!), and to explore their body.

We'll return to self-touch over the next chapters when we explore in more detail how bodies work, including orgasms, and when we talk about sex in relationships. It's incredibly important not to shame ourselves, or the other people in our lives, for self-touch and solo sex, instead allowing ourselves and others space and privacy for it. Obviously, this can be a difficult thing to navigate and negotiate in some relationships.

Solo sex and self-touch can be just as good as – and sometimes better than – doing things with other people. It's an important thing to make time for if it is something that you enjoy. Sometimes people feel like they need permission because of all the negative messages around masturbation, so – should you need it – please have our permission to wank!

FANTASIES, EROTICA AND PORN

Similarly, people's experiences of fantasies – sexual or otherwise – are massively diverse. We know many people who've simply never had a daydream or fantasy, to the extent that the whole idea doesn't make a lot of sense to them. We also know people who have a vivid fantasy life, which is a deeply important aspect of their everyday life and which would be a huge loss if they ever couldn't do it. We're reminded of the scene in *When Harry Met Sally* where Harry describes a complex sex dream in detail, and Sally offers in return her surprisingly simple recurring dream in which 'a faceless guy rips off all my clothes'. Of course, there are people whose experiences are every-where between these two poles.

Some people prefer to draw on other people's fan-tasies, for example, by reading erotic fiction, looking at images or watching videos. Others can come up with their own scenes, images or stories quite readily in their heads. Many like to mix it up, bringing in other materials sometimes, and going it alone at other times. Many people find it enjoyable to make and share stories, images (drawings or photographs) or videos, online or with selected friends.

For some people, a fantasy can be as simple as imagining – or looking at – a certain part of a person's body. At the other end of the spectrum, it could be a detailed ongoing story, set in a complex world full of characters whom they have created or borrowed from other people's stories (TV programmes, novels and the like).

MULTIPLE EXPERIENCES: WHY PEOPLE FANTASISE
The motivations for fantasising are incredibly diverse, for example:

- 'One thing I get out of fantasising is that, when I look at an image of a woman and imagine her desiring me as much as I'm desiring her, it's a turn-on, and it also makes me feel a bit sexier in myself.'

- 'Sometimes when I'm walking along listening to music, I fantasise a kind of music video montage in my head, maybe with famous people or partners. It feels sexy but not explicitly sexual, and I like the swagger and confidence it gives me.'

- 'I found fantasising – and writing down my fantasies – an incredibly helpful way of figuring out what I was into sexually. The frisson of actually putting it down on paper was really exciting, as was sharing it with some of the people I had sex with.'

- 'I sometimes find fantasies really helpful to imagine doing things that I don't feel confident doing in everyday life. For example, I often imagine dominating people in fantasy, but that's not something I ever have the nerve to do in reality!'

- 'For me, fantasy has taught me some really important things about myself. For ages I imagined kind of rescuing this character who was being bullied in my fantasies (and then doing all sorts of rude stuff to him!). Eventually I realised that this character was part of me. Maybe the fantasy enabled me to be kind to a part of myself that I struggled to be kind to in real life. That realisation was hugely helpful.'

- 'For me it's really simple. I just remember a sexual encounter I've had – run it through in my mind – and that gets me off.'

You can see from these examples that sexual fantasy can be anything from fairly mundane – if enjoyable – to hugely psychologically meaningful. Just as psychotherapists sometimes invite people to reflect on their dreams, fantasies can tell us a lot about our hopes and fears. They can be a way of dealing with the tough stuff that's happened to us. You might find it helpful to reflect on your own fantasies in this way.

try it now SEXUAL DESCRIPTION OR FINDING SOMETHING THAT YOU LIKE

If these ideas about fantasies sound interesting to you – or if it's something you already do – try writing down one of your fantasies (just a paragraph description will do) or drawing a picture of it. How does it feel to put it down on paper?

If you're somebody who prefers to draw on other people's materials, then try finding something that appeals to you (if it's safe for you to do this kind of search). Online the most popular sites are the tube sites of free videos and images. However, they often depict a fairly limited range of people and practices. You might like to look at other sites – which may involve paying for the work involved in creating them – that include specifically feminist, queer, alternative (alt), body-positive, kink or LGBT people and practices.

In terms of erotica, you might look at:

- Classic books of fantasies, such as Nancy Friday's collection of real women's fantasies, *My Secret Garden*, or Emily Dubberley's more recent book of the same, *Garden of Desires*.

- The vast array of erotica online. People write sexual fan fiction about pretty much any combination of film/TV characters you could imagine. ('Archive of our own' is one place that collects these, for example.) There are also videos and images of this kind of thing.

- Sex bloggers who write about their own experiences. (Girl on the Net is a good one, for example.)

Start looking and you'll probably find something that appeals to you.

WHAT IF I'M FRIGHTENED OR WORRIED BY WHAT TURNS ME ON?

One thing that people can struggle with, when doing an exercise like this, is the fear that they will find out they have desires which don't feel okay in some way. Fantasising, looking at porn and erotica, and solo-sex can lead us to thoughts and feelings that make us uncomfortable, either during or afterwards. We might find ourselves wondering: 'What does it mean that I feel turned on by that?', 'Am I a bad person for getting off on that thing?' or 'How can I enjoy a fantasy that is so different to who I am in everyday life?'

The first important thing to remember is that fantasy and reality are two very different things. It is okay to think about whatever you like. Imagining yourself eating a big slice of cake is not the same thing as actually doing so. Most people have things that turn them on sexually which they wouldn't want to do in reality, perhaps because they are impractical, or other people wouldn't be interested, because they wouldn't be consensual, or because they just wouldn't be as exciting in real life as in their heads.

If it's simply that the thoughts and feelings you find yourself having are generally considered weird or unusual, there's no problem with that. It's important to remember that people actually find a massive range of things erotic, and it shouldn't matter how common or uncommon it is. It's probably the case that there are other people out there who have the same desires as you, with whom you could talk about them. The internet can be a great place for finding people with similar interests. There are communities for most sexual interests, identities and activities. Also it's a great idea to bring in some self-care after you've been fantasising or looking at porn or erotica, so you have a chance to reflect on what has happened and look after yourself if there have been any surprises.

Of course, if you find yourself really troubled by what you're fantasising about, perhaps to the point that it starts taking over a lot of your time, or you worry that you might act on something that isn't consensual, then it is definitely worth getting support. There are therapists and other professionals who are very sensitive to these issues, as well as charities that specialise in these areas.

There's a difference between fantasies and fiction, and images and videos of real people. When you're imagining something, reading a story or looking at pictures that somebody has drawn, everybody involved has consented (yourself and the author or artist who has put their work out there). However, photographs and videos of people may or may not be produced consensually. For example, some clips and pictures online have been taken without the person having been aware it was happening. Or they may have been forced or pressured into it, or the clip or photograph could have been stolen from elsewhere. Also, sometimes an individual who can't consent, like a child or animal, is being filmed or photographed. It's a really good idea to reflect on what you're looking at and whether you can be sure it was consensually produced. There is a lot of stuff that is explicitly ethical and consensual, and it will feel a lot better – for you as well as for the other people concerned – if you focus on that.

If you think that the desires you have in your fantasies, erotica-reading or porn-viewing are something that you *would* like to act out, then a vital question to ask yourself is whether that can be done consensually. We'll be coming back to this question in plenty of detail in Chapter 5.

TUNING INTO OURSELVES

You've seen that it can be really hard to get in touch with what turns us on because of all the messages we've received about what is and isn't okay when it comes to sex, self-touch and fantasy. Hopefully, we've given you some practical ideas about how you might become aware of some of these messages and how to hold them a bit more lightly, as well as how you can look after yourself, be present to yourself, and tune into your desires and sensations.

We'll now look more closely at how we can apply these ideas to our relationship with our bodies in particular.

CHAPTER 3
Bodies

So, there are lots of different kinds of sex that people may enjoy. In the last chapter we considered a lot of the more psychological and social reasons why people might like different things, such as their personal experiences growing up, or the kinds of sexual images they saw around them. Sex is biopsychosocial – our physical reactions are intertwined with these experiences. So, for example, we might have seen an image of a certain kind of sex and found it exciting personally, and that might mean that our bodies now become more aroused when we do that thing.

Of course we can't completely tease these things apart, but it's worth exploring the biological element in more detail. Another reason that people like different things is that all of our bodies are unique: working in somewhat different ways from each other. And they work differently at different points in our lives.

Because bodies are diverse, it is useful to assume that the body in front of you (when having sex with another person or people) will always be different from your own – and from other bodies that you may have encountered! Different body parts might work differently for different people; so, it's worth exploring what we individually find physically pleasurable, and the different kinds of arousal and pleasure that people experience in different kinds of sex. Our bodies also change over time, and this has implications for the kinds of activities we might enjoy.

DIVERSE BODIES

A lot of mainstream sex advice tends to be limited in the information it provides about bodies. It often focuses on certain parts of the body (especially the genitals) and how they function, whereas we're going to be thinking about the whole body and all of the parts that we can enjoy touching or having touched.

Sex advice often accepts that bodies can be different, but tends to focus on the differences between genders, with a big emphasis on how men and women have very different bodies. Actually, everybody's body is different, and other things are often just as important as – or more important than – gender. There is a lot of diversity within each gender in terms of how people's bodies work, as well as similarities between people of different genders. So, for example, two people of different genders who really enjoy spanking might have more in common in terms of areas that they enjoy having stimulated and sensations that they enjoy, than two people of the same gender who have very different tastes.

The other thing that some sex advice focuses on when it comes to bodies is specific groups of people. There are whole books and chapters on how disabled people, older people, pregnant people, fat people or trans people have sex – as if sex were a very different issue for them because of their 'different' bodies. We think it's more useful – and more enjoyable – to adopt this approach for *everybody* rather than just for these specific groups. We don't only have to learn what is different about a new person's body if they come from one of these groups, we have to learn what's different about *any* new person's body, because every body is different.

Sex tends to be much better if we go in with the assumption that everyone's body looks different, works differently, feels different, and responds differently. We could even go so far as to say that every encounter involves a new body, given that the same person's body feels different on different occasions. It's a great idea to go into sex each time prepared to learn how this body works (both your own body and the other body or bodies involved).

MULTIPLE EXPERIENCES: DIFFERENT STROKES FOR DIFFERENT FOLKS!

Here are some examples of different preferences, which often run counter to our, or others', expectations of what might, or 'should', constitute pleasurable experiences:

- 'Someone was giving me a blow job and putting my penis deep into their mouth and sucking really hard, even when I said that I prefer a softer, lighter touch on the tip of my penis. I think they must have read a load of the stuff that's out there about how to give the perfect blow job, but that's not what works for me at all.'

- 'As a woman, when I started having sex with women in my thirties I assumed it'd be much easier than having sex with men because their bodies would work in the same way as mine. With the first woman I slept with I went straight for the kind of finger penetration and g-spot stimulation that I enjoy, and she was horrified! Turns out we're a lot more diverse than I realised.'

- 'People often lick and kiss my ear because they've heard that's a good erogenous zone. Actually, I do enjoy it, but only on my right ear, as I'm deaf in my left. So, I have to explicitly ask people to do that.'

- 'My body definitely responds differently at different times. Sometimes I enjoy light tickly sensations, but sometimes that's too much and actually feels unpleasant. I really like it when a partner gets that and checks out how it feels on a particular day, rather than getting huffy that his tried and tested "technique" isn't working this time.'

- 'When I was heavily pregnant, the doc told me that I shouldn't have sex lying flat on my stomach, which is how I usually do it, even though it felt okay. Actually, it was quite a good opportunity for me and my partner to try some other things.'

If we accept that everybody's body is unique and different to everybody else's, it can be good for us in two ways. First of all, it can make us feel better about all our own physical idiosyncrasies, rather than worrying that they somehow make us weird or abnormal. Second, it means that we'll probably be a better sexual partner for other people because we won't be making assumptions about how they work, but will be up for discovering their body and what they enjoy.

WE ALL NEED TO REMEMBER: EVERY BODY IS DIFFERENT

This idea of diverse bodies can be quite challenging to hear, especially if we were hoping that we could just learn a few techniques and skills that would work for everybody and make us seem like a good lover. It's important to remind ourselves that we're all in the same boat with this: we all have different bodies, and every sexual encounter will be with somebody with a different body.

What we're going to give you in the rest of this chapter, and the rest of the book, are the skills to work with this fact of life, rather than pretending that you ever could find a one-size-fits-all way of doing sex.

PARTS OF THE BODY

Many parts of the body enjoy different kinds of touches and sensations. Some of these feel erotic or sexual, some not, and some do or don't depending on the context or timing. For example, you might like some parts of the body touched in certain ways but not immediately – only after some build up.

If you pick up a standard sex manual and look up bodies, you will generally find that most of that topic is devoted to genitals and how they work. This is because, as we've seen, most sex advice assumes that sex means penis-in-vagina (PIV) sex. Therefore, it focuses on penises and vaginas. Also, it generally assumes that all penises will work in very similar ways, and all vaginas will work in similar ways.

While genitals are sexual parts of the body for a lot of people, for some people they aren't the focus at all, and many of us have other parts of the body that are as – or more – important sexually.

try it now BODY MAP

Something you could try is drawing an outline picture of your body and then ticking and crossing where you might and might not like to be touched. You can use your discoveries from this to have more enjoyable solo sex and to inform your discussion with partners about what you do and don't like.

Some people have a pretty good idea of this from experience of touching themselves – or from others touching them. For others it's a pretty new idea. So, don't worry if you're not sure in places. Also, it doesn't have to be a very accurate drawing; something like a stick figure or gingerbread person is fine!

You could draw yourself with or without clothes on (or both). You could draw yourself front and back. You could use a different coloured pen for where you like touching yourself and where you like being touched by another person. It might be useful to see where those are the same and where they are different.

You could take this a bit further. As well as ticks and crosses, you could put question marks or a mark out of ten for how much you enjoy it; you could add notes about when and where you would like this, about how things might differ if you had all your clothes on or off, or how you might feel in different kinds of relationships or mental states (e.g. if you were feeling more confident or less certain).

If this is something you'd like to share with somebody else, there is more in the next chapters about how you can go about doing this, perhaps making it part of a larger 'sex menu' about your likes and dislikes.

MULTIPLE EXPERIENCES: ENJOYING THE BODY

Here are some examples of the kinds of bodily touch different people enjoy.

- 'Feet are easily the most erotic part of the body for me. I love finding shoes that look amazing and having somebody else devote lots of time to my feet

– massaging them, giving me a pedicure. It's amazing having a partner who finds feet as erotic as I do.'

- 'I used to get quite disappointed during sex because as soon as my cock was hard, people would go right for that. I do need to have my cock stimulated if I want to come, but I like to spend a lot of time having other parts of my body touched first: my belly, thighs and other parts of my pubic area.'

- 'As an asexual person, I really enjoy physical contact with my partner, but it's important for both of us that it's not sexual. Generally, for us that means a lot of cuddling, stroking each other's arms and hair, that kind of thing.'

- 'It's a cliché that the brain is the most important sexual organ, but for me that's definitely the case. Reading erotic fiction online is far more exciting than sex with another body for me. While I do touch my genitals in order to come, it's only very briefly through my clothes at the point at which I'm already totally aroused.'

- 'People tend to assume because of my body that I'm going to want loads of foreplay, but really once I'm turned on I prefer to get on with it. For me, that means having my clit touched in some way – going down on me is the best. That's not to say I don't like other parts of my body to be touched at the same time. It's amazing if they grab hold of my arse or thighs while they're doing it.'

- 'My best kind of sex is anal sex – being on the receiving end. It makes me come harder than any other kind of sex without any other touch being necessary; although I do like the feeling of another person's body on top of mine – that makes it really intense.'

GENITALS

Strange as it may sound, genitals aren't always central to enjoying sex. Other parts of the body, as we've seen, can be just as important, and more so. But genitals are surrounded by so many taboos and assumptions that they can be quite a mystery to us, both other people's and even our own. We don't tend to see genitals much, except in very specific places – like pornography – which tends to focus only on genitals that look and work in a very particular way. For that reason, it's worth spending a little time getting to understand how our own genitals work and thinking about the different ways in which other people's might work.

The advice we generally receive about genitals often suggests that they all appear and work in the same ways. This can lead to a lot of shame if our genitals don't work in that way, or if we don't have the kind of genitals that are being described. For example, when it comes to the appearance of our genitals – as with bodies more generally – there is a very narrow ideal about how they should look which very few people actually match up to. Other people can easily exacerbate our own shame about genitals that don't match this ideal by making jokes or even cruel comments. In reality, there is a huge variety in size, shape, hairiness, how much skin there is and how it's formed, smell, taste, smoothness or roughness, and many other aspects. Instead of people feeling that they should change their genitals to match some ideal, or feeling bad if they can't, it would be great if there were more awareness and acceptance of this diversity, and a sense that all genitals – like all bodies – are beautiful in their uniqueness.

Another important issue is that, for many years, sex advice set out an ideal that women should be able to orgasm from being penetrated alone. Sex manuals often search for sexual positions that could enable that to happen. However, we know that around 70 per cent of women need external clitoral stimulation in order to come, and most of them are never going to get the stimulation they need from PIV sex. This can lead to feelings of failure, or putting up with kinds of sex that feel uncomfortable or unpleasurable because of the sense that you *should* be enjoying it.

Similarly, there's a lot of fuss about 'g-spot' (internal) orgasms, including claims that they are a better kind of orgasm than other sorts. People can, therefore, feel bad if g-spot stimulation does nothing for them, or if it's actually unpleasant or painful. The focus on penetration also means that there is a widely held assumption that penises should orgasm while they are penetrating another person, without requiring other kinds of stimulation. This can be shaming for the large number of people who don't enjoy that, or find that they orgasm in other ways.

There are also many people who:

- Don't have the kinds of penises, vaginas or clitorises that are generally described in sex advice.

- Have penises that can't easily penetrate a vagina or anus because of size or shape.

- Have vaginas that don't self-lubricate enough, or at all, for penetration, or that tense up if they attempt it.

- Don't have much or any sensation in their genital areas, have health conditions or medications which affect lubrication or erection, or have other aspects of their bodies which make certain kinds of genital stimulation easier than others.

- Have genitals that can't easily be classed as either a penis/scrotum or clitoris/vulva, or have had changes made to their body during their lives which means that their external clitoris or penis has been altered or removed.

Despite how common these experiences are, they can leave people feeling ashamed and anxious about having sex.

Sadly, the solution that much of the media comes up with in response to these issues is simply to ignore anybody whose body doesn't fit a narrowly prescribed type of genitals that work in a particular way. We only hear about all these other kinds of experiences in sensationalist articles or programmes about 'embarrassing bodies', things going wrong, or groups of people who are portrayed as exotic and different. A far better approach is to assume that *all* genitals look different to each other and *all* genitals work in different ways. Very few people indeed will have the kind of genitals that you might see in sex advice or porn, or ones which work in exactly the ways those genitals do, all of the time. The Great Wall of Vagina and the Crash Pad Series are examples of an art exhibition and porn site that do show diversity of genitals.

Because all genitals are different, a good starting point is to get to know your own genitals and how they work. As always, a key thing here is to try to step away from all the messages you've received about how they *should* look or feel and tune into how they actually are – while recognising that this is often really difficult because of how powerful those social messages are.

try it now TUNING INTO YOUR GENITALS

Here are two activities for exploring how your genitals look and feel. Because of all of the cultural baggage that we've mentioned, diversity of sexual/asexual experience, and painful sexual experiences in some cases, not everybody will feel comfortable engaging with their genitals so directly. As always, these activities are optional, and you should never push yourself further than you feel comfortable. If you'd like to do an activity but not something so direct, you might try drawing, or making a plasticine model, of how your genitals feel to you, or describing the sensations you have in that area in writing. If you do experience sexual arousal, you might create two drawings, models or paragraphs comparing how your genitals feel when you are turned on versus the rest of the time.

Starting with how your genitals appear, you could spend some time looking at them with a mirror or with a phone camera (you don't have to actually take a photo unless you want to). If you like this idea, you could try to see the whole area rather than focusing on one part of it. Going back to the idea of 'being present' that we covered in the last chapter, see if you can suspend any idea of an 'ideal' set of genitals to which you might compare them, and instead just notice what yours are like. For example, you might observe the different colours and textures in the different areas, where hair grows and where it doesn't, how they smell, or any changes that happen as you're observing and touching them (e.g. swelling, hardening, moisture).

Moving on to how your genitals work, you might spend some time exploring how your genitals feel in response to different kinds of stimulation. You could try fantasising or engaging with porn or erotica and seeing what impact that has. You could spend some time touching parts of your body in ways you enjoy and noticing how genital – and other – sensations shift. You could also try touching the genitals directly and noticing how they respond to different kinds of stimulation (direct and indirect, harder and softer, dry and lubricated, external and internal, etc.). Make sure you pay attention to the whole genital region rather than just focusing on the parts that often get the most attention. A lot of people find touch pleasurable on the tops of their thighs, for example, or on their labia or perineum (right in the middle of the area between the genitals and the anus), or around the anus itself. Just be cautious not to go from touching your anus to touching other areas without washing your hands, as that can introduce infections.

The focus in a lot of sex advice is on how different genitals are between men and women. There are often completely different sections on how men's genitals work, and how women's genitals work, as if everyone within those categories worked in exactly the same way, and as if there were huge differences between men and women. The second assumption behind a lot of these messages is that men's and women's genitals are complementary – which gives the message that 'proper' sex happens between a man and a woman, and involves a penis penetrating a vagina. There are many problems with that assumption, given that sex can happen in all gender combinations, and also because many men and women don't particularly enjoy PIV sex, or enjoy other things just as much. The strong emphasis on PIV can lead people to assume that anybody with a penis will want to use it to penetrate, and anybody with a vagina will want it to be penetrated during sex. It can also lead to people doing PIV even when they don't enjoy it or find it uncomfortable or painful. We need to challenge the tyranny of PIV as the only 'good', 'natural' or 'normal' way to have sex!

The assumptions about genitals here are both wrong: first that within the categories of men and women, people's genitals all work the same, and second that men's and women's genitals are complementary. Actually, there's a huge amount of diversity in the way different genitals work within people of the same gender, and there is also a lot of similarity between the different genders in relation to genital function – basically because that part of the body all begins in the same way when we're foetuses and only goes in different directions relatively late in the developmental process. The clitoris and the penis are basically the same thing. Both have a glans (a sensitive outer part with lots of nerve endings); both have a shaft of erectile tissue (which fills with blood, swells and throbs when we become aroused); both extend backwards through the body from the base. Everybody also has PC (pubococcygeus) muscles in their genital region which contract if they have orgasms – and can be pleasurable to tense and relax at other times. The main genital difference is really just the extent to which the shaft is external or internal.

A lot of people also assume that there are major differences between men's and women's genitals in terms of whether they ejaculate, or whether they become aroused by penetration, but in fact many women ejaculate when they are aroused, and many men are stimulated by penetration. This is because of the location of both the prostate and the internal parts of the clitoris/penis.

It's vital to attend to the specific set of genitals you are dealing with, rather than making any assumptions about how they will work based on gender – or anything else. You simply can't assume that this person will enjoy penetration, or will like to be touched in a particular way, or will experience orgasms or ejaculation. All of these – and more – are things that you need to find out. Just as your experience of your own genitals is unique, theirs will be too.

try it now   DRAW YOUR OWN GENITALS

You might wonder why we haven't included a drawing here, given that it might help to show you where the different bits are that we've been referring to! The reason is because we think it is so important that you discover your own genitals and how they work. Any kind of diagram implies that certain areas are most important – because of which bits get named or drawn and which don't.

If it's something that you'd like to do, it can be more useful for you to make your own drawing of how your own genitals look and feel to you, and to use your own words to describe the different areas that are important (whether those are more biological terms, slang words or labels that you've made up yourself). Like genital touch, however, this kind of activity isn't for everyone. In fact, one of us finds it really useful, and the other one doesn't get anything out of it. If you're interested in finding out more about how different genitals work, and the diversity of sexual anatomy, then check out Cyndi Darnell's website and videos (in the resources at the end of this book). Justin's BishUK website also has a bodies section which provides a lot more detail about genitals and how they work.

MULTIPLE EXPERIENCES: GENITAL SEX

To give you even more of a sense of the variety of genitals and the way they can work, here are some example experiences from people who enjoy genital sex of some kind – but for whom it has very different meanings.

- 'I really enjoy getting fucked deeply by large penises or dildos. I find that sometimes I get so wet from that that I need to dry off a little before continuing because it gets too slippery.'

- 'I love penetrating people. I don't have a cock that is part of my physical body but that's no problem. Sometimes I have such a strong sense of having a cock that the imagining of that – while I'm on top of my partner – is enough for both of us. Other times I use a strap on.'

- 'Sex for me used to always just be about a penis in a vagina but I became increasingly conscious that the other person was doing it because they thought they had to, and I was doing it because I thought I had to. It's actually pretty limiting what a cock can do when it's inside a vagina.'

- 'I enjoy vaginal and anal sex but, for me, neither of those holes lubricates much on its own so I definitely need extra lubrication. The key to good sex for me? Lots of lube!'

- 'For me fucking with fingers and hands is way more pleasurable than anything else. They are just so much more dextrous. Fingers can touch very specific spots inside my body, and the experience of having someone's whole hand inside me is the most intense connection I've ever had with another person.'

WE ALL NEED TO REMEMBER: BE PATIENT WITH OURSELVES

Tuning into our own bodies and genitals when we receive such strong messages about how they *should* look and what they *should* do is extremely difficult. The fact that this is an area where there is so much taboo and so little information or opportunity to talk about it makes it even more challenging. It's good to be patient with ourselves and not to try to force ourselves to think or feel differently – recognising that this will probably be a long journey, not something we can shift overnight.

PLEASURE AND WHAT WE MEAN BY IT

Just as people often assume that sex means penis-in-vagina intercourse, they often assume that the point of sex is to get an orgasm. This means that we can often focus only on sex providing one specific kind of pleasure, and we can get very goal-focused about sex – trying to 'achieve' an orgasm, or to 'make' another person have one.

It's not that orgasms aren't important. For many people they are a very pleasurable experience. Also, historically, it has been assumed that sex is only about some people having orgasms (e.g. men but not women, not disabled people, not older people, etc.). So, it can be really important to claim the right to experience orgasms during sex if they are something we enjoy.

However, even though there's a really strong cultural pressure to have them, no-one can really agree on what an orgasm even means! Also, orgasms are not the *only* kind of pleasure that people can experience; many different kinds of orgasms – and other kinds of climax – are possible. We'll give some examples of this in a moment. Finally, focusing on one specific goal in sex often takes us away from pleasure rather than towards it. There can be so much pressure to perform a certain kind of pleasure during sex that we lose touch with what we're actually feeling and why we're having sex in the first place.

Let's take a step back now and think about all of the different reasons why we might have sex. This can help to expand our understanding of all of the different things that we *can* get from sex, and how orgasms are only one possibility.

THINK ABOUT IT: YOUR REASONS FOR SEX

For this activity, you might like to write down a list that you can return to, or you might just like to think about your answers. If you can, it's worth taking a little time over this because you might well come up with more possibilities once you've exhausted the more obvious reasons.

Remember the last few times you had some kind of sexual or physical contact, or erotic experience (whether alone or with another person or people). Why do you think you did it? What were your motivations at the start? Of course, it might well be that there were several different things driving you, including aspects of what you were looking for and what you were hoping to offer to somebody else.

Then think about what you – and anybody else involved – actually got out of the experience. That may or may not be the same as what you were expecting or hoping for. What did the experience give you? How were you left feeling afterwards?

Broadening it out further, think about all of the reasons why you think other people might seek out sexual or physical contact, or erotic experiences, and all the things they might get from this. What are all of the different possible reasons you can imagine, whether or not you've experienced them yourself?

WHY DO PEOPLE HAVE SEX?

You can probably see – from your answers to the activity – that there are lots of different reasons for having sex. Not everybody is looking for the same things from sex, not everybody gets the same things out of it, and people's reasons also change a lot over time – they might be different at different ages and in different relationships, for example.

When we've done this activity with people in workshops, they have come up with a vast array of different reasons. Here are just some of them. You might find it useful to underline any that you can remember applying to you, or add them to the list you made.

excitement,

to get an orgasm,

to feel comfort,

to feel wanted,

because somebody has asked you to,

to feel attractive or desired,

not wanting to lose the relationship,

distraction from other things,

boredom,

as a form of exercise,

to get money,

so the other person will then owe you something back,

to feel good in your body,

because you feel like you're supposed to do it,

to put your partner in a good mood,

pity,

to try something new,

for a sense of connection,

intimacy,

to feel powerful,

because you're angry,

because you don't want the other person to feel rejected,

out of frustration,

to learn more about yourself,

for fun,

to pass the time,

guilt,

to get pleasurable sensations,

to act out your fantasies,

to wake up,

to experience sides of yourself that you don't otherwise,

for the afterglow,

relaxation,

because you know somebody else expects it,

validation,

stress relief,

confidence,

because it's your routine,

procrastination,

for release of tension,

to feel a sense of proficiency – like a good performer,

to reinforce your masculinity/ femininity,

to try to heal wounds from the past,

to prove something,

to get pregnant,

to reassure the other person,

experimentation,

to reaffirm a relationship,

to stop thinking about everything,

to cheer yourself up,

to stop the other person from pressuring you,

to feel 'normal',

because you've got free time,

as an act of rebellion,

to get it out of the way,

to make somebody like you,

to let go,

to show somebody how skilful you are,

to help you fall asleep

Of course, different people generally have different reasons for having sex – and our reasons vary from time to time. It may well be that if you're having sex with somebody else you're each looking for different things from it. We'll come back to this when we consider how you might communicate what you're hoping for, as well as when we look at how to have sex consensually when all these different reasons – and sometimes pressures – are in play.

When we realise all of the different needs and desires that we might be looking for sex to fulfil, we can see that we're often asking sex to do a lot for us! It can be a high pressure situation, beyond even the expectation to get and/or give an orgasm. It can be a bit like a major celebration (such as a birthday party, wedding or religious holiday) where everyone involved is hoping for so much that there's stress, conflict or a feeling of being let down when it actually happens.

On the positive side, if we can actually recognise all of the different things that somebody *can* get from sex, then we can focus on experiencing different kinds of pleasure from it, instead of feeling like sex is a success if orgasm is 'achieved' or a failure if it isn't. We can also recognise that another person might be enjoying it, whether or not they're having orgasms, erections, ejaculations, etc. For example, maybe this time what we're hoping for from sex is to feel connected to our partner, and what they're looking for is some fun and light-heartedness after a stressful day. In this situation, it may be that sharing something new – and a bit silly – will meet both our needs without genitals or orgasms necessarily being involved.

CLIMAX

As well as reasons for sex in general being massively diverse, there is actually a similar diversity when it comes to orgasm (if this is something that we enjoy). There are many different kinds of orgasms possible; there are lots of different possible routes to having an orgasm; and orgasms mean very different things to different people, and at different times.

If you've had orgasms yourself you might well have noticed some variety in the experience – for example, on a spectrum from mild to much more intense, or fleetingly pleasurable to a longer-lasting sense of fulfilment. The following examples give you some sense of the different kinds of orgasm or climax that are possible to experience in a variety of different ways.

MULTIPLE EXPERIENCES: DIFFERENT KINDS OF CLIMAX

- 'An orgasm can be quite a perfunctory thing for me: I'm a bit bored, I have a wank, it's a nice release but nothing more.'

- 'Sometimes orgasms can be really intense: those times when I know it's coming and I can relax into it – not needing to force it in any way – I can slow it right down and properly enjoy it. Then it's wave on wave of pleasure and I'm often left laughing about how great I feel.'

- 'Occasionally I get this thing with orgasm which is like what I get with intense physical exercise as well – they call it a 'coregasm', I think! It's like I feel completely in my body, and it feels very strong and powerful, this energy surging through me. I feel capable of anything.'

- 'There's a climax like an orgasm for me when I'm having a sexual fantasy. I run the story through in my head and there's a peak moment in there – like when a character comes, or when two characters kiss for the first time, or something like that – and that's a similar sensation to an orgasm for me but all in my own mind: a braingasm!'

- 'In order to get an orgasm – for me – I have to really go into myself. Like, I have to shut my eyes and just focus on the sensations inside. It can be great, but difficult if I'm with a partner who wants to talk a lot during sex or to be looking at each other when it happens. That's just not something I can do.'

- 'Being kinky, the kinds of climax I enjoy during a scene don't always involve an orgasm, or genitals at all. During sensation play, there's often a build-up of feeling – from being caned or paddled, for example – which gets more and more and more intense until it reaches a peak, and then slows down to a stop. Sometimes that peak involves a release, like breaking down in tears, or a massive sense of connection with the other person, or a huge sense of pride of having endured. There's definitely an afterglow after that.'

- 'For me there's a kind of climax that comes when the person I'm with orgasms. I can feel so connected to them that their excitement and breathing and tensing and releasing is like my own. Even though my body isn't in that same place, I feel it right alongside them.'

- 'My partner has these really intense climaxes which happen really quickly and several times in a row – sometimes as many as seven or eight times. While it's really cool to be with someone who can have multiple orgasms – there's a real buzz from that – it can be difficult if it goes on long after I've come myself. We've started making our own ending point because otherwise it could just go on forever!'

- 'I recently went to a tantra workshop where they got us to have a breathgasm. I was seriously sceptical! It involved breathing deeply into different parts of our bodies in a kind of cycle, and also making a lot of noise and thrusting our hips while lying on the floor. I enjoyed letting go into that situation, but I knew that I wasn't doing the things that my body needs to actually have an orgasm. Towards the end we sped up the breathing, tensed everything, and then relaxed.

And I was totally shocked because I felt the exact same way I feel after a genital orgasm!'

- 'I hate the way that people think that ejaculation and orgasm are the same thing. Like, because I can ejaculate, some partners will assume that I need to do that in order to have really enjoyed it. Or, on the flip side, sometimes I do ejaculate but I haven't actually come – and they stop there.'

A climax can be experienced as so many different things. It can be a mechanical release, a demonstration of masculine or feminine sexuality, a relief of stress, a loss of control, allowing someone to see you at your most vulnerable, a display of intimacy, the height of physical pleasure, a transcendent spiritual experience, a performance demonstrating prowess, a giving of power to another, an exertion of power over another, a form of creative self-expression, a humorous display of our rather ridiculous humanity, an unleashing of something wild and animalistic, a deeply embodied experience, an escape from bodily sensations and pain, a moment of really feeling alive or free, and many other things. Of course, this means that people vary a lot in terms of whether they want an orgasm, or not, and under what conditions.

So, there are many different kinds of pleasures and climaxes that people can get from sex, erotic situations and physical contact. Spend some more time reflecting on which ones resonate for you. You could write your own statements, like the Multiple Experiences quotes, about the physical and emotional pleasures that you've experienced. You might find that they are a bit more complex and rich than you previously realised.

WE ALL NEED TO REMEMBER: DIFFERENT THINGS FOR DIFFERENT PEOPLE, AND AT DIFFERENT TIMES

People can experience pleasure without sex, sex without climax, and climax without orgasm. Also, people can have sex – including climaxes or orgasms – which isn't pleasurable at all.

It's important for us all to remember to tune into ourselves and what we find pleasurable or fulfilling, rather than assuming that we *should* have sex, or *should* experience the sex we do have in particular ways. It's also vital to remain open to the ways in which other people experience things, rather than making assumptions about how they will work, or placing expectations on them.

CHANGE OVER TIME

A common myth about sex is that it should remain exactly the same over time: our bodies should continue to work in the same ways sexually; the same things should give us pleasure; and we should continue to want the same amount, and type, of sex. This is often tied into the assumption that sex is necessary for our relationships and for our general health and happiness. Plenty of people have no sexual attraction, or have no sex in their relationships, and are definitely happy and healthy that way.

Discrepancies in sexual desire between partners, and fluctuations in desire over time, are perfectly normal (which we'll say a lot more about in the next chapter). Bodies in particular change over time, and these changes too are perfectly normal.

If we can be present to our own bodies, we often notice that we enjoy many different kinds of touch and that we experience many different kinds of pleasure and/ or climax. If you can observe that, then you might already have seen the changes which are constantly happening: in your own body and in other people's bodies. You can realise that change is not problematic, or anything to worry about, but rather change is an inevitable part of life which we can embrace. It can be exciting to discover our body anew each time we're sexual or physically intimate. Every time is like a first time if we can remain open to the possibilities of how our body – and other bodies – might be on this particular occasion, rather than trying to force them to be the same as they have been before.

try it now HOW YOUR BODY CHANGES OVER TIME

Think about your bodily changes over the following time periods. How do you notice that your body changes over the course of an hour, a day, a month, a year, a decade or a lifetime? Think about both *objective* changes (e.g. losing an erection after ejaculation, having a particular illness), as well as how you *felt* in your body (e.g. buzzy, tired, warm).

Hour

You might like to consider an hour during which you had some form of sexual, sensual or erotic experience. Perhaps note how your body changed before, during and after the experience.

Day

Consider how your body changes over the course of a day from when you wake up to when you go back to sleep. Pay particular attention to sexual experiences and how they relate to other aspects of your bodily state.

Month

You could think about the month just gone, or you might like to keep some kind of record over the coming month, taking some notes every day. Notice what's going on with your body each day of the month and how it feels for you, as well as noticing how that relates to the sexual side of your life.

Year

Think back over the past year. What changes have happened in your body during that time? This might include changes that have happened to it, like having an illness or accident, and changes you have made to it, like starting a physical activity or getting a tattoo. What changes happened, and how did they influence how you felt in the body? What relationship did you notice between that and your sexual, sensual or erotic experiences?

Decade

Reflect back over the past decade in a similar way. There may have been more major changes during this period, for example, moving from adolescence to adulthood, having a child, becoming disabled, recovering from a major illness, or making changes to your body to reflect your gender – or other – identity. How did such major bodily shifts feel? How did they relate – if at all – to your experience of your sexuality?

Lifetime

Finally, allow yourself to reflect back over the whole course of your lifetime in a similar way. Were there any big turning points in terms of how your body worked, or how you experienced it? What about the future? What kinds of changes are likely to happen, and what impact might those have? What are your hopes and fears about potential bodily changes and how they will relate to your sexual, erotic or sensual experience?

Something that you may well have noticed in this activity is that some changes are temporary, whereas others are permanent, and also that changes can involve losses and/ or gains in terms of how you experience sex and sexuality.

MULTIPLE EXPERIENCES: BODILY CHANGES AND SEX

These example experiences give you a sense of the kinds of things, and changes, that people experience over the course of shorter and longer periods of time.

- *Hour:* 'I know people say you're meant to feel really sleepy after sex, but that just doesn't happen to me. I might not be able to have another climax, but I still really really enjoy touching my partner and being touched after orgasm, or having sexy conversations about what we've just done and what we might do next.'

- *Day:* 'I noticed when I woke up this morning that I started to have a wank because that's always been my morning ritual. Halfway through, I realised I was kind of just doing it because I thought I should do it when I could fit it in. I decided to stop and wait till I actually felt horny. That ended up happening a couple of times later on in the day (luckily I work from home!), and it was a lot more enjoyable. I also noticed how my body felt – and responded – differently the time when I was really awake and the time when I felt more snoozy.'

- *Month:* 'I've chatted a lot with my mates about the ways our periods affect our sex lives. It's surprisingly diverse. I've definitely noticed a peak of horniness in the middle of the month – which I guess is when I'm ovulating – but some of my friends are horniest before, during, or after their periods. One of them said that orgasms really help with period pain.'

- *Year:* 'I started doing sex work earlier this year. I've noticed quite a few changes in my body since I've been having sex more – and in more different ways. I'm definitely fitter than I was! Also, I was surprised by how sometimes it can be sexually pleasurable for me – and some clients are really keen on that – when other times that isn't a part of it. But, then again, that was the case before I started doing sex work too – sometimes it's about pleasure, and sometimes it's about other things.'

- *Decade:* 'The major thing for me in the last ten years was discovering the ace (asexual) community. Before that I'd been feeling so bad about the fact that I didn't experience sexual attraction. I tried to make myself do it a couple of times but then pulled back because it felt so wrong. Finding the ace community AVEN online was this huge relief. And I noticed my whole feeling about my body shifted after that. I felt easier and more relaxed – like my body was my friend instead of my enemy. It feels particularly good when I'm around other ace people dancing and hanging out.'

- *Lifetime:* 'Around fifteen years ago I was diagnosed with MS. One of the earliest things I noticed was how it became increasingly difficult to orgasm in the intense way that I used to. This was a major loss for me and my partner, and it was so frustrating that none of the medical staff took it seriously because they never seemed to want to talk about sex. Over time we discovered sensation play – using gadgets like clamps and pinwheels – something we'd never really done before but which gave us back a more intense connection which works for how my body is now.'

If you reflect on your own experiences, and these examples, you can see that our bodies are always changing, moment by moment and over periods of years and decades. Instead of expecting our bodies to work in the same way in the evening as they do in the morning, the same way when we're under the weather as when we're 100 per cent, or the same way at age 60 as they do at 30, it would be great if we could be more open just to how our bodies are now.

This is about being okay with ourselves, whether or not we actually feel sexual, as well as recognising that we might enjoy – and not enjoy – different kinds of touch on different occasions. It's about acknowledging when some options have closed down to us – as in the last example – and it's also about being open to any new options which may have opened up with the bodily changes that have happened. While it's definitely important to let ourselves feel the losses that come with ageing, illness and accidents, for example, it can also be useful to notice what different possibilities follow major bodily changes. It's helpful to recognise both the temporary and permanent shifts that accompany various changes: often there are elements of both because nothing stays the same for ever; however, we're also never exactly the same person that we were before the change.

APPEARANCE AND ATTRACTIVENESS

One of the things that makes bodily change over time a great deal more difficult for most of us are the social messages that we receive about bodies and ageing. We live in a culture which idolises youth and also gives us incredibly restrictive norms about what an 'attractive' body should look like. For this reason, we often feel terrible if bodily changes shift us away from this in any way, and this alienates us from our bodies, rather than enabling us to stay embodied (or within our bodily experience).

For many people, worries about how they look are one of the biggest things that get in the way of being present when they're having sex, and that get in the way of enjoying sex – because they're so distracted by these kinds of critical thoughts. For example, we've spoken to lots of people who will only have sex in certain positions and with low light because they're so fearful of a partner seeing their 'muffin top', 'bingo wings', scars, veins, bones or 'cellulite'; because they think that they have a small penis, flat chest or big belly; or because they generally see that their body doesn't match up to cultural ideals of being young, slim and toned, and judge it in comparison. With these kinds of appearance concerns, we don't even think to blame all the restrictive norms and ideals about what makes somebody attractive but simply go straight to blaming ourselves for eating 'too much', not working out 'enough', being lazy or lacking willpower. It's easy to get into an increasingly painful self-critical cycle that takes us away from enjoying our bodies at all. Instead of our bodies helping us to enjoy sex, it feels like they're getting in the way of it.

So, what can we do about it? The first thing to remember is that it's not easy. As with the cultural assumptions about being normal, or having 'proper' sex, it's very hard to completely step away from the ideas we receive about what bodies should look like and how important it is to be physically attractive. So, we mustn't give ourselves a hard time when we keep slipping back into judging how we look in the mirror or worrying about how we appear to a partner. If we're not careful, it's easy to move from beating ourselves up for how we look to beating ourselves up for caring so much about how we look!

Here's a useful thought experiment: What would it be like if we put as much time into trying to be kinder towards our bodies, or feeling good about them, as we currently put into trying to change our bodies, or feeling bad about them? There's a great line in the Tim Minchin song 'Not Perfect' which hints at this: 'And the weirdest thing about it is, I spend so much time hating it, but it never says a bad word about me.'

BEFRIENDING OUR BODIES

One thing that we can do is put some time and energy into befriending our bodies. A good way to do this is to think about the times when we feel connected with our bodies, as opposed to the times when we feel separated off from them and judge them critically. For example, some people feel that sense of wholeness, or connection, when they're doing a fun physical activity (like dancing or swimming), when they're out in nature, or when they're doing other physical things that they find pleasant (like being in a hot tub or going on a fairground ride). Of course, those things will work for some people but will do quite the opposite for others – you may well have thought this as you scanned those examples if you hate camping or rollercoasters as much as we do! The important thing is to find what works for you: the times in your life when you feel on friendlier terms with your body – or at least you're less aware of feeling bad about it.

try it now

Try writing a list of the times, places and situations where you feel most connected with your body.

Now think about how you might build a little more of this kind of scenario into your life, and notice what impact that has over time. As with all the changes we've been talking about, it's likely to be slow and gradual, not a sudden overnight shift. Perhaps start by planning a time to do one of the things you've listed in the next fortnight.

As well as planning in time to be kinder towards your body, other things that some people find helpful include getting angry and active about all the negative cultural messages that exist around our appearance. It can be good to turn our criticism out towards the things that make us feel so bad about our appearance instead of inwards on ourselves. For example, you could get together with others to discuss these things, or make a zine or blog post about it (we include more on this in the resources at the end of the book). You could also try to dial down how much you say critical things about other people's bodies (whether friends, family members or celebrities) and about your own body, in order to model a kinder approach outwardly. You might find it helpful to engage in events and spaces where there are more diverse bodies around to expand your own ideas about what kinds of appearance can be beautiful. For example, there are body diverse club nights, dance classes, fitness groups and hangouts in many cities. Some people find saunas and naturist spaces great to see diverse naked bodies. Those can be interesting alternatives to going to a gym, slimming class or standard nightclub. Some of the further resources at the end of this book give more ideas.

When it comes to sex, how can we best approach it, given that we probably don't always feel great in our body and physical appearance? If you do want to have sex, but you're feeling very low on body confidence that day, it's fine to do things like dimming the lights, keeping some clothes on or getting under the covers.

In terms of a longer-term approach, it's useful to apply some of the ideas from Chapter 2 about 'being present'. When you find those critical thoughts about your body coming in, try slowing down and breathing, acknowledging that they are there but trying not to grasp onto them and get dragged along by them. It can be helpful to remember that those ideas come from the wider culture, rather than from you, and also that they affect all of us – including the person or people that you may be sexual with. Take yourself gently back to all of your senses instead of focusing only on the critical thoughts. For example, focus on how you're feeling in your body, what you can see, smell, touch, hear and taste. Of course, this doesn't always help, and if you do find yourself sinking into a really tough feeling, it's fine to stop sex and do something kinder to yourself. We'll talk more in the next couple of chapters about how you might communicate at such times with the other person, or people.

WE ALL NEED TO REMEMBER: CRITICAL OUT, KIND IN!
It's important to keep an eye on the messages around us about bodies and sex, and to reflect on the ways in which they affect us and the other people in our lives. It all goes back to treating ourselves, and our bodies, kindly and to tuning into what makes us, and our bodies, feel good.

Given that our bodies change so much over time, it's a great idea to keep returning to the body map that you did earlier and revisiting it, remembering that what we like is not once-and-for-all. As we'll see next, this kind of change is actually positive – rather than negative – because it helps us to remember that each time we're sexual we're a slightly different person and body to the last time, and that will mesh slightly differently with other people we're engaging with, which can be really exciting.

Relationships

So far in the book, we've mostly focused on your own individual relationship to sex, but you've probably already found yourself wondering about how all of that works when other people are involved. Sex can happen in a number of different relationship contexts. Here we'll explore all of these contexts in which sex can happen, to widen our understanding in a similar way to the way we've expanded our understanding of what counts as sex. Then we'll think about who sex is for, and how it can work when more than one set of desires, expectations and anxieties is in play.

We'll challenge a common assumption about sex in relationships: that people should always mesh perfectly in terms of the amount and type of sex they want, and that this should stay the same over the course of the whole relationship. Actually, it is completely normal to have discrepancies and fluctuations in sex in relationships, and this should be expected. Taking that perspective can really lift the pressure off and open up other ways of negotiating these kinds of differences and changes.

The idea of being present, which we introduced in Chapter 2, is also important when it comes to sex between people. So, we'll work on how to be present in relationships towards the end of the chapter.

DIFFERENT CONTEXTS FOR SEX

Mainstream sex advice books mostly seem to be aimed at people in couples who are struggling to keep having enjoyable sex in their relationships. There are also some books aimed at single people, but most of those assume that they are looking to form a long-term sexual relationship with another person while having a few casual sexual relationships along the way.

You might well find that you fit into one of these descriptions – long-term relationships or dating – and we're going to be saying a lot more about having sex in these contexts over the next two chapters. However, it's useful for everyone to remember that these aren't the only relationship contexts in which sex happens. For some people, neither of these scenarios describes the main way in which they have sex. For others, expanding the possibilities for sexual relationships can be a good way of addressing sexual problems – or it can open up new and exciting opportunities.

The core message here is that sex can happen in all kinds of different contexts, and that is fine!

THINK ABOUT IT: THE CONTEXTS OF SEX

Reflect on the kinds of contexts in which sex can happen and with which of those you're personally familiar. For each of the following categories, consider the different ways in which you've experienced sex or relationships and how you've found them. You might also think about the kinds of sex or relationships that you've fantasised about, but not tried, under each category and whether these are things you'd like to try in reality or not.

- Number of other people involved (from zero to many)

- Type of relationship in which sex happens (e.g. strangers, friends, monogamous partners, non-monogamous partners)

- Level of connection (from a one-off to a close, ongoing connection)

- Level of sex involved (from none to sex being the main thing you do together)

- Physical context in which sex happens (e.g. online, outside, in bed, etc.)

Let's look at each of these with a few more ideas about the different contexts that *can* be involved and what these are like. You might like to keep reflecting on which ones appeal to you and which don't.

NUMBERS OF OTHER PEOPLE INVOLVED

Perhaps the most common thing to come to mind when you imagine sex is sex with one other person. Sex advice

– and other mainstream media – generally puts across the view that the only normal, healthy way to have sex is in a monogamous couple, so it's not surprising that this is what we often think of. We've kept emphasising that solo sex can be just as fulfilling, enjoyable and 'proper' as sex with other people. Additionally, of course, it's possible to have sex with more than two people. One of the most common sexual fantasies is some kind of 'threesome' or 'threeway', where you have sex with two other people at the same time. And there are also various forms of group sex, from two couples having sex together, to an orgy with a room full of people, and everything in between.

We could see sex with more than one person on a kind of spectrum. It's not just that we either have sex only in a monogamous couple or we're having orgies every night! Activities that might be somewhere on the spectrum include, for example:

- Watching porn as a couple

- Touching yourself on a train where other people *might* be able to overhear you, or realise what you're doing, but probably not

- Having sex with a partner with the curtains open, or within earshot of other people

- Going down on someone in a toilet at a pub

- Fucking in a field

- Dancing, snogging and grinding with people at a nightclub

- Going to a sex party and having manual sex with a partner in a room where other people are also being sexual

- Filming yourself having sex and putting it online anonymously

- Arranging for someone to come and join you and your partner for sex.

As well as reflecting on which of these you find exciting, you might find it useful to think about where your own boundaries are: which might you be up for in reality and which wouldn't you? People have different reasons for this, of course; for example, some are excited by the idea of 'getting caught', whereas others find that a massive turn-off. Some people are more turned on by the idea of seeing other people being sexual, some more by being seen, some neither and some both.

Of course, there are also ethical and legal issues around consent in some of these situations where a person could inadvertently find themselves involved – at least as a viewer – in a sexual scenario. This is very important to consider, and we'll explore it more in Chapter 5.

TYPE OF RELATIONSHIP

There are, perhaps, two key aspects to the kind of relationship in which sex occurs: first, the kind of relationship it is and second, whether it is sexually monogamous or non-monogamous.

In terms of the kind of relationship, in addition to romantic partnerships, sex can happen – for example – between strangers, between friends, between a client and a professional, and between ex-partners.

In any of these relationship contexts there can be an agreement between the people involved about whether they are sexually exclusive or whether they can also have sex with other people. Sexual monogamy, or exclusivity, is another thing that it's useful to see on a spectrum:

Spectrum of sexual exclusivity

Monosex

Polysex

*No physical
intimacy
at all outside
this relationship*

*Open to sex
with multiple
people*

For example, at the left-hand end of this spectrum would be relationships where it's not acceptable to hug, kiss or flirt with anybody other than your partner. Moving along the spectrum, we might have relationships which are open to partners reading erotica or watching porn, but not doing anything sexual with another person. Then we have monogamish relationships, where perhaps it's okay to snog another person or do certain sexual activities but not others. There might be rules around those arrangements, such as 'Don't ask, don't tell,' 'Only if you involve me too,' 'Only with somebody of a certain gender' or 'Never with the same person twice.' Towards the right-hand end, we might have forms of swinging or open relationships, such as couples who meet singles for sex and vice versa. Then we might have polyamorous people of various kinds: solo poly people who are open to having multiple partners but consider themselves their own main partner, or poly networks where several people have sexual relationships with each other. Some polyamorous people have relationships which are romantic as well as sexual, some which are just romantic, and some which are just sexual.

Have a think about where you are currently on this spectrum. Where have you been on it in the past? Where would you like to be, or imagine being in the future?

LEVEL OF CONNECTION

In addition to the level of sexual connection, there are also different levels of emotional connection that we can have with sexual partners. We hear a lot about sexual couple relationships which are also close emotional relationships: maybe that is the culturally 'ideal' sexual relationship. However, we've already talked about how the *sexual imperative* – that partner relationships *must* be sexual (page 12) – can be damaging. And many authors have written about how it can be hard to get sex and emotional closeness in the same relationship. For example, sex and relationship therapist Esther Perel says that it's often tough to have a relationship which is both hot (passionate) and warm (involving everyday intimacy).

So, it's also helpful to think about the level of emotional connection and intimacy that we have. We can have sex in relationship contexts anywhere on a spectrum from having no emotional connection with the person (e.g. strangers or people we don't like very much) to having a close, ongoing, emotional bond, and everything in between. Demisexual people usually only have sex in a relationship where there is a strong emotional bond. Aromantic people generally have no desire for that kind of romantic relationship with anybody.

LEVEL OF SEX INVOLVED

We've talked elsewhere in the book about asexuality and the spectrum of sexual attraction that people experience: from none to high levels. It's useful to bring this idea of a spectrum into our thinking about the relationship context of sex – or other kinds of physical contact between people. So, when you think about the various relationships in your life, you could think about the role that sex plays in each of them. There will be relationships in which there is no sexual component at all – for example, asexual relationships, non-sexual friendships, etc. There may be relationships in which sex plays a major part – for example, relationships with ongoing sexual partners, or seeing a fuckbuddy or sex worker purely for sex. And then there may be many kinds of relationships that fall between these two extremes. Consider, for example:

- Relationships with friends and colleagues where there's an element of flirtation on which you'd never actually act

- Friendships where there's a lot of touching and cuddling, on the borderline of being sexual

- Friends and/or exes with whom you very occasionally end up having sex

- Mates with whom you watch porn or go to strip clubs

- Being a sex worker who has sex with clients, but where there's also a strong element of emotional support

- Your relationship with someone whose erotic fiction you read online.

For some people, the level of sex involved is a really important factor in distinguishing different kinds of relationships – such as for people who treat sexual partners very differently to how they treat their friends. For others, the boundaries are a lot blurrier. For example, a relationship anarchist is someone who doesn't make much distinction between the importance of romantic partners, sexual partners and friends.

PHYSICAL CONTEXT IN WHICH SEX HAPPENS

As well as assumptions about relationship context, people often assume that sex generally happens in a certain physical context: in a bed, in a bedroom, and between two people who are both physically present. Any other kinds of sex are often seen as ways of 'spicing up' a relationship, rather than being potential, everyday forms of sex in their own right.

From some of the examples we've mentioned, you can see that offline sex can happen in many different physical contexts: fields, dancefloors, trains and parties, and you can probably think of many more.

There are also many different ways in which people can have sex when they aren't physically present with each other, whatever relationship they have. These include: phone sex, webcam sex, sexting, cybersex over instant messaging apps, or sending each other erotic letters. Of course, all of these examples open up the possibility that people could be in different places, even to the point of being on opposite sides of the world. They may or may not ever meet in person.

Forms of online sex and sex-at-a-distance also begin to open up the possibility of having sex with people across different points in time. For example, if you watch porn, read erotica or check out somebody's sex blog, you're engaging sexually with them at a different point in time than the point at which they put it out there. This really expands our understanding of what sex *is* because it means that a person could give another person an erotic moment or orgasm several years after doing the stimulation – even after they themselves are no longer alive!

Hopefully this has helped you to reflect on the different contexts in which sex can happen – and perhaps to expand your own ideas about the contexts in which you would be interested in having sex or other forms of contact. It's useful to keep these possibilities in mind as we explore sex in relationships in greater depth.

WHO ARE WE DOING THIS FOR?

One major point to bear in mind about having sex with another person – or people – is that there will often be more than one *reason* for having sex. In Chapter 3 we looked at why we have sex and came up with lots and lots of different reasons and motivations – of which we may be more or less consciously aware. Here are some examples of the similarities and differences that can be present when people are having sex with each other.

MULTIPLE EXPERIENCES: SIMILAR AND DIFFERENT REASONS FOR HAVING SEX AND PHYSICAL INTIMACY

- Greg and James have been friends for some time and have recently realised that they're attracted to each other. They didn't really talk about what exactly they were going to do, so when they did have sex they defaulted to anal sex. Both of them expected that it was what the other one wanted or what 'counted' as 'proper sex'. However, actually, Greg would have rather done something kinkier but less penetrative, and James's preference is for oral sex.

- Kim and Sidra met Alex online on a website for couples seeking singles for threeways. They exchanged messages back and forth for a few weeks about the kind of sex they were looking for and what they got out of it. They realised that their fantasy of Kim watching Sidra have sex with somebody else and then joining in meshed well with what turned Alex on, so they got together. Alex also made it clear that they'd like some relaxed time cuddling afterwards and, although that wasn't essential for the other two, they were happy to do it.

- Jo and Mark are a married couple who have been living together for three years. Last night they had sex, partly because Jo wanted reassurance that she was still attractive to Mark, and Mark that he could still perform well sexually.

- John hasn't been to a sex worker before. He gets in touch with Paula and they arrange to meet. When they're discussing what it is that John would like, John says that he really wants to do what Paula enjoys doing. This is a bit tough for Paula – although it sometimes happens – because for her sex work is a transaction and the sex that she has for enjoyment happens outside of her job.

- Freddie and Veronica have been together for twenty years. Sex has never been an important part of their relationship, but they do always make time at the weekend for the kind of physical affection that they both enjoy most. Freddie really loves being cuddled in bed and read to by Veronica, as it makes him feel very safe and connected together. Veronica is a long distance runner and loves for Freddie to massage her when she gets back from a run.

People's reasons for having sex sometimes mesh more than others. Sometimes a lack of mesh is a problem, and sometimes it isn't. Sometimes it's possible to find a kind of sex or physical contact that fits with what everyone is looking for, even when they're each looking for different things. Other times the different reasons for sex mean that people are actually looking for things that are incompatible or too different to accommodate.

Of course, in all of these situations, people's

motivations for having sex or other kinds of contact are likely to change from occasion to occasion. For example, feeling that they 'should' have a certain kind of sex at a certain frequency because they're in a relationship might remain a background issue for Jo and Mark, and for James and Greg, but it might be in the foreground more on some occasions than on others. When they're particularly relaxed or turned on, reasons such as fun and horniness might come to the fore more, or they might feel more able to go for the kind of sex that they really feel like having.

NAVIGATING DIFFERENT REASONS

Two things are helpful when trying to navigate the various different motivations that are in play when we're with another person, or people.

1. Try to be cautious about any 'shoulds' or 'oughts' that you – or others – are feeling (e.g. 'We should have sex because we haven't done it for a while,' 'I ought to have this kind of sex because everyone else is,' 'I'd better have sex once a week or they might dump me,' 'I must find a sexual partner because that's what normal people do.').

2. Try to tune into what you – and any others involved – actually want, and why, as much as possible.

Both of these steps are difficult when we're surrounded by so much pressure to have certain kinds of sex for certain reasons, so we need to go easy on ourselves and on the people we're having sex with. It's understandable that we sometimes find it really hard to know what we want or why, or to articulate it even when we do. Hopefully, you'll now have started to challenge some of your assumptions and will have started to tune into yourself, laying the groundwork for communicating your desires, anxieties and uncertainties to somebody else.

DOING IT FOR YOURSELF/DOING IT FOR THEM

It's extremely common for us to make assumptions about what another person wants sexually, based on what wider culture tells us, on what they've seemed to enjoy before, or on our expectation that they'll want the same things we do. So, for example, we might have expectations that all people of a particular gender, or all people with a certain body type, will want sex in the same way. We might assume that because somebody has always seemed to like a particular activity they'll always want us to do that during sex. Or we might think because we enjoy being touched or kissed in certain ways, so will another person.

So, we can often end up having sex more for another person than for us – based on a rather narrow set of assumptions about what they'll want, rather than on what they actually want. In that scenario, it could easily be the case that nobody is enjoying sex as much as they might (as in the examples of Greg and James, and Mark and Jo, earlier).

Hopefully, when we're embarking on sex, what we really want is for everyone involved to enjoy it as much as possible: ourselves and the other person or people involved. However, it's easy for this to get complicated by our assumptions about what's okay and what's enjoyable.

It may well be that one of the things we enjoy is seeing another person enjoying themselves, and vice versa. This can create a great upward spiral of enjoyment as we each get off on the other person getting off. However, it can be problematic if one or more people start to feel under pressure to demonstrate just how much they're enjoying everything – even if they're not – or if our own enjoyment becomes lost because we're so focused on the other person having a good time.

Some partners resolve these issues by making different people the *focus* of sex on different occasions – 'This time we're going to focus on your pleasure, and next time on mine.' Particular activities which are more explicitly about giving and/or receiving (like oral sex or massage) can be useful for this. Alternatively, it can be useful to keep checking in with yourselves about whether the sex you're having is valuing each participant's desires as highly, or whether it might have tipped more in one direction and needs re-balancing. In the next chapter, we'll say more about how the various power dynamics between people can make this tricky – and how you can go about raising your awareness of this.

WANTING AND NOT WANTING SEX

As well as there being multiple reasons in the mix every time we have sex, it's likely that some parts of us will want it and some parts of us won't. This is true for most decisions that we make in life, such as whether to go to a party, whether to take on a certain job, or whether to meet someone for coffee. For example, if it becomes clear that we might have sex tonight, part of us might be drawn to that because of being horny and wanting the connection to another person and the stress release feeling it'll bring. Another part of us might resist it because we're a bit tired, we're not quite sure exactly what we want to do, and we'd also like to finish the book we're reading.

So, what do we do? The important thing here is to give space to both these sides of yourself: the side that's drawn to having sex and the side that isn't. What we often do under these situations – because uncertainty can be so difficult – is to shut down one side entirely and only listen to the other. That often means that the other side becomes louder and more difficult to handle. For example, if we have sex without listening to the side of ourselves that doesn't want it, we might find it hard to focus or feel resentful about it.

It's great to check in with ourselves and think, for example, 'Okay, around 60 per cent of me is up for this, but 40 per cent isn't, so I'm going to go ahead, but also will acknowledge the part of me that's tired and not so interested.' Maybe that would involve saying to yourself that you'll let yourself have a lie-in tomorrow, or you'll build in some time to finish reading your book over the weekend. Or you might reach a compromise of having a kind of sex which is quicker or more relaxing than what you had been planning. Even in the situations where it's more like 99 per cent wanting sex and only 1 per cent not wanting sex, it's still way better if we can acknowledge the 1 per cent.

THINK ABOUT IT: WANTING/NOT WANTING SEX

Remember back to the last time there was an opportunity to have sex – or another form of physical contact – with another person. Draw a rough pie chart of the proportion that you wanted, and didn't want, to go ahead. Try writing on each side of the pie chart some of the reasons why you were drawn towards doing it, and towards not doing it.

Think about whether you acknowledged all of these 'pros' and 'cons' on that occasion. How might you allow yourself to do so more in future?

There are many reasons why people have sex. These are often very powerful, and we can feel that there's a lot at stake. For example, we might feel like the whole relationship rests on it, or that we aren't an okay person unless we do this thing. It also may well be the case that part of us wants to have sex and part of us doesn't, all at the same time. And, of course, that will be true for the other person or people involved as well as for us.

In all of this complexity and uncertainty, if we really don't want something, or if we're very unsure of whether we want it or not, it is absolutely fine – in fact, vitally important – not to go ahead. Having sex that we really don't want, or are very unsure about, can be bad for us in several ways: it's an unkind way to treat ourselves; it often leaves us enjoying sex even less than we did before; and the other person or people can feel terrible when they realise that we weren't really into it. For the same reasons, of course, it's equally important to create a situation in which the person or people we're having sex with can say if they don't want to, or aren't sure.

It's vital, then, to tune in as much as possible by asking ourselves: 'Do I really want to do this?' This is both a form of self-care and a way of treating ourselves consensually.

WE ALL NEED TO REMEMBER: DON'T HAVE SEX WHEN YOU DON'T WANT TO
If you really don't want something – or are unsure whether or not you want it – it is vitally important not to go ahead.

DISCREPANCY AND FLUCTUATION ARE NORMAL

People tend to believe that the 'ideal' sexual relationship involves people wanting the exact same kind of sex, and around the same amount. People are often concerned about the average number of times couples have sex, assuming, for example, that they should match up to it, and that there's a problem if they don't. Sex manuals tend to cover the same kinds of sex, as if there were a universal one-size-fits-all kind of sex that everyone should be having.

However, major research studies in this area have found that – contrary to popular belief – people in relationships generally *don't* have the same level, or types, of desire. For example, the British National Survey of Sexual Attitudes and Lifestyles (NATSAL) found that, at any one time, one in four people who are in a relationship don't share the same level of interest in sex as their partner(s). Over the years that means that everyone will probably have this kind of discrepancy at some point. Indeed, another big survey – the Enduring Love study – found that levels of interest in sex changed a lot over time for people in long-term relationships: fluctuation is the norm. Importantly, neither discrepancies nor fluctuations seemed to make much difference to overall satisfaction with the relationship.

So, in our relationships we should expect to have differences in sexual desire, and we should expect everyone's desires to change over time, both in terms of levels of desire and the kinds of things that turn us on.

DISCREPANCIES

It can be useful to think about our sexual desires in relationships in terms of where we overlap and where we are separate. If you have a sexual partner of any kind, try making your own diagram – like the Venn diagrams below – representing how much overlap, or distance, you think there is. Then write down the kinds of sexual experiences you both/all enjoy (in the overlapping part) and the kinds you each like individually that the other(s) doesn't share (in the separate parts of the circles). You might find it useful to return to the list of activities you made in Chapter 1 to remind you of things to include on the diagrams.

Because of all the pressure to have exactly the same desires, it can be hard to navigate the separate areas on these diagrams. Far too many people still feel guilty about having desires that a partner doesn't share, especially if they're less culturally accepted. And far too many people try to get a partner to stop having a desire if it's not something that they themselves like the idea of. One way people often do this – sadly – is to dismiss something their partner likes as not 'proper' sex.

WHAT ISN'T SEX?

We've spent a lot of time in this book thinking about what sex is. Before going on, just think for a moment about the opposite question: What *isn't* sex? What activities or practices can you think about which are never, ever sexual for anybody in the world? Make a list of everything you can think of.

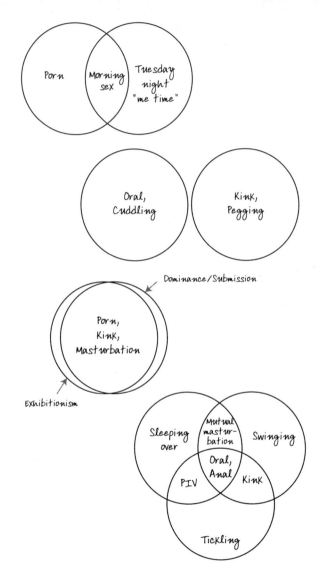

Hopefully, what you've learnt from this is that pretty much anything has the potential to be sexual. There's a joke about the rules of the internet: rule 34 is that 'If you can think of it, somebody will have made porn about it.' On this point, sociologist Gayle Rubin provides useful advice to keep in mind when we're thinking about the sex discrepancies that we will inevitably have in any relationship:

> *Most people find it difficult to grasp that whatever they like to do sexually will be thoroughly repulsive to someone else, and that whatever repels them sexually will be the most treasured delight of someone, somewhere ... Most people mistake their sexual preferences for a universal system that will or should work for everyone.*[4]

It's vital that we don't impose our sexual preferences on a partner as if they're a universal system, just as much as we don't impose what we imagine to be 'normal' or 'proper' sex on ourselves (see Chapter 1). This can be particularly important if a partner is into something that is already culturally regarded as 'abnormal' – they may well already have a lot of shame around it, to which we don't want to add. As with tastes in food, it's easy to slip from 'You

---

[4]   Rubin, G. (1984). Thinking sex: Notes for a radical theory of the politics of sexuality. *Social Perspectives in Lesbian and Gay Studies: A Reader*, 100–133.

like this food, but I don't' into 'Urgh! How could you possibly like that?!'

A couple of useful ideas from kink communities on this point are YKINMKBYKIO (your kink is not my kink but your kink is okay) and 'squick', a word for something that you find to be a turn-off or uncomfortable while still recognising that other people can enjoy it.

It's absolutely fine for you not to do something if it's not what you're into (in fact it's vital), but it's also important not to judge anybody else because they're into it. Of course, in some situations it can be that a partner's desires are so different to yours – or such a squick for you – that you don't feel able to be in a sexual relationship with them. That's fine, but what isn't okay is shaming them for it. It's about valuing everyone equally, rather than valuing one person *over* the other person or people. It's possible to have a lot of love and attraction for somebody but no overlap in what you're into sexually. If sex is an important aspect of a relationship for you, then this would be a time in which you need to re-evaluate the relationship. In the next chapter, we'll say more about how you can navigate discrepancies and meet the sexual desires you don't share.

FLUCTUATIONS

As we've seen, fluctuations are the norm in relationships. If you're sexual with somebody for a while, the kind of thing you'll want to do with them, and the amount you'll want to do it, will certainly change. The Enduring Love study found that for many people in long-term relationships sex tailed off completely, and that was fine.[5] For others it ebbed and flowed over the years. For some it became more important and fulfilling as time went on.

Here are just some of the reasons why our levels of desire, and the kinds of sexual activities in which we engage, can change over time in a relationship:

Chronic pain, acute pain, illness, changing ability; wanting different things; getting bored of things we're doing; bereavement, trauma, mental health issues; having kids, kids leaving home, trying to get pregnant; relationship conflict; discovering new things about your body/sexuality, gender changes, ageing, changes in sexuality; fancying partner less/more/differently, fancying someone else as well/instead, interest in porn/erotica, experiencing something with someone else (e.g. another partner, sex worker, fuckbuddy); being diagnosed with an STI; change in living situation, work or other everyday stress; change in sleep patterns, how you feel about your body; having sex and something going wrong – such that you're worried about doing that again; experience of something non-consensual.

5   Barker, M.J. & Gabb, J. (2016). *The Secrets of Enduring Love: How to make relationships last.* London: Random House.

You might want to go back to the Venn diagram you made and fill it in over time: either looking back over the course of your relationship and how it has changed and/or, in an ongoing relationship, filling it in every year or so from now.

Different people have different rules in their relationships which allow for different responses if their fluctuations lead to them having greater discrepancies than before. For example, non-monogamous people may be able to meet some of their desires with other partners (in some of the different contexts we explored in the first section of this chapter). Rules around solo sex, porn, erotica and fantasy are also important here.

EVERY TIME IS A FIRST TIME

In Chapter 2, and earlier in this chapter, we talked a lot about the concept of 'being present' to yourself, and how you might cultivate that in general and in relation to your sexual feelings. It's about staying with your whole experience: being open to what is drawing you towards having sex and also what is drawing you away from it.

The idea of being present can also be a very helpful way of navigating the particular difficulties involved in having sex with another person, or people – which involve multiple sexual desires as well as our thoughts about what their needs are, and their thoughts about what our needs are, and our assumptions about what their thoughts about our needs are, and so on.

When we get into these kinds of thought spirals, it often feels easiest just to go for default 'safe' forms of sex, such as those that are most culturally accepted, or those that we've done a lot of times before with this person (or both). While this can make it a less anxious experience, it can also be less exciting and fulfilling, with less potential for discovery or creativity.

An alternative approach to cut through these thought spirals is to focus on being present to the experience as it unfolds. When we're each caught up in our expectations and assumptions about another person, we're not really connecting to them. And when we're basing what we're doing on a set of 'shoulds' and 'oughts' we're not really connecting to ourselves either: we're too distracted by all these ideas about 'proper sex', what we 'should' be doing, or how the other person or people might react. Being present is about foregrounding connection to both ourselves and others.

Key elements of being present include:

- Trying to stay *in the moment*, rather than planning what you're going to do next or worrying about what just happened.

- Trying to be with the *whole* of your experience, rather than focusing on certain feelings, thoughts, sensations or body parts. For example, the sex you're having might bring up multiple feelings of excitement, boredom, amusement, frustration and horniness. It's about trying to be with all those feelings rather than focusing on one of them, or trying to keep hold of the 'positive' ones and get rid of the 'negative' ones.

- Slowing down and paying attention to the *granular detail* of what's happening. For example, not just 'she's sucking my nipple' but trying to experience all the different sensations that involves: warmth, pressure, moisture, sounds, smells, what it looks like, etc.

You might want to remind yourself of other aspects of being present which can apply during sex (page 42), but hopefully this gives you a few ideas. It's also useful to remind yourself how hard it can be, and how important it is to be gentle with yourself, rather than letting 'I'm not being present enough' become another critical thought that's going around your head!

In many ways, this is a bit like making every time we have sex like a first time because we're coming to the experience anew: without expectations, with curiosity and with an openness to surprising ourselves.

It's interesting that a lot of sex advice advocates doing things to 'spice up' your sex life, which aims at introducing this kind of element of uncertainty and surprise. For example, sex advice often suggests doing new things, surprising each other with sexual scenarios, trying new positions or even pretending to be strangers.

Of course, you might like to try any of these things as ways of being more present to each other, but there's also the simpler way of slowing down and tuning into the experience. In a sense, whenever we have sex we are always a different person, and so is the other person (or people if there are more than one). We've seen how both our bodies and our sexual desires change over time. Being present is about recognising the new person in front of us, even when they're someone we've had sex with a hundred times before, and about recognising the new person in front of them!

If this seems useful to you, you might like to try the 'every time is a first time' approach next time you have any kind of sexual, erotic or sensual interaction with another person. The activity on being present in Chapter 2 gives you the general idea, but in this case it is the sensations and feelings during sex that you're using as the anchor to come back to each time you become distracted, rather than the breath (although, of course, your breathing will be part of that experience).

MULTIPLE EXPERIENCES: BEING PRESENT TO SEX

Here are the experiences of other people trying this approach, to give you some further ideas about how it might work, and some of the challenges involved:

- 'When I used to get blow jobs, I was more into the excitement that I was getting one – and how it looked – than how it actually felt for me. After going to a few yoga classes I learnt how to notice all the different sensations in my body, from the tips of my toes to the tips of my fingers. I started applying that when having a blow job and found that it was totally different – like a whole different plane of experience!'

- 'For me, this idea of being present was really useful because I spent a lot of the time when having sex with my partner worrying about whether it was okay that we were doing the same thing we often do, feeling like I should take control more, wondering what he wanted, and thinking about how long it was going to last. Now, when I have those thoughts, I don't try to block them out or get angry with myself, but I try to focus on what I'm feeling in my body, noticing how it changes over time.'

- 'I used to love cuddling with my partner, while we watched TV or before we went to sleep at night. Over the years, though, it just became something we took for granted, I think. Like, we'd both be focused on something else when we were doing it. We decided to try being present to it again to see what that was like. We switched off the TV and just focused on cuddling. I was noticing how it felt to snuggle into the nook of their arm, the scent of their body and the warmth of their skin, how enclosed and safe I felt.'

- 'I've found it particularly useful to slow down when my partner is masturbating me. Before, I'd always kind of tense up and speed up, racing for the climax, and sometimes it would disappear because I was trying so hard. Now, I deliberately play with slowing down my breathing and really feeling the way his fingers move – different to how I touch myself. Something about that is hugely horny, and the slower orgasm has a different quality to it which is intense in a way I enjoy.'

try it now BEING PRESENT TO AN EXPERIENCE WITH ANOTHER PERSON

As you can see from the examples, it can be really challenging to bring this approach to sex, given just how many expectations and assumptions are often loaded onto that experience. You might want to start with a less loaded form of physical contact – like a hug, a handshake or a snog. What's it like to slow down and notice the experience, being present to it, rather than moving straight on to the next thing?

Of course, treating every time as a first time can be scary – in the same way that all first times can be scary – because it comes with that uncertainty about what to do and how another person will respond. If we treat every body as a new body – even one we're familiar with – then we don't know how it will respond to our touch. However, there is an excitement that comes with it, if we can be open to that scariness.

This approach can be really helpful in part because it can focus our attention on consent. It's easy to slip into having not-very-consensual sex when we assume that everyone will enjoy the same things, or that the people with whom we're sexual will enjoy something now because they enjoyed it in the past. The every-time-is-the-first-time approach means that we get used to continually checking in with people, rather than making those kinds of assumptions. We'll say a lot more about how you might do this in the next chapter.

This may seem quite awkward or frightening at first because we're often so used to defaulting to certain kinds of sex and don't really tune into ourselves or others. However, if we can make this kind of tuning in and being present our new habit, we often find that sex becomes more enjoyable, more connected, safer and more consensual than it was before.

Communication and Consent

Over the course of this book, we've explored the different kinds of sex and physical contact that different people prefer, how every person's body is different, and how sex means something different to us all. In the last chapter, we explored how these differences play out when we're actually having sex with another person, or people.

Mainstream sex advice has some awareness of these challenges, but it tends to respond to them by just saying that we need to talk with our partners about sex. However, it often gives very little advice other than 'We know it's awkward, but you've got to do it'! Here we aim to give more practical tips about how to actually go about communicating about sex with sexual partners, especially in relation to ensuring that the sex you're having is consensual.

WHY CONSENT IS THE CORE OF EVERYTHING

We've noticed in mainstream sex advice that consent is hardly ever explicitly mentioned. When we looked through the bestselling sex advice books, the average number of pages devoted to consent was 0.005 per cent! It seems like the authors buy into the wider cultural idea that consent isn't really relevant: as long as nobody is actively expressing distress about sex, then it has been consensual. There's a baseline assumption that of course the sex that partners have will be consensual. This is linked to the myth that non-consensual sex only happens between strangers where one person is deliberately trying to force another person into sex.

These assumptions give sex advice a kind of permission to then tell readers that they must do sex in a certain way, and at a certain frequency. For example, a lot of books suggest that partners have sex once a week on a particular day, whether or not they're in the mood. Many books advocate surprising your partner with sexual scenarios without checking whether they like the idea. And several say that you need to provide certain kinds of sex to a partner even if you dislike, or hate, those activities.

In this way, the implicit assumption in sex advice that all sex will be consensual allows them to suggest some very non-consensual things.

The danger is that this kind of advice adds to an already very non-consensual culture around sex, where people feel pressured to have sex for all kinds of reasons other than actually wanting it – as we've explored throughout this book. It's easy for us all, as readers of sex advice, to internalise these assumptions and therefore not to question whether the sex we're having is consensual (both for ourselves and for others involved).

WHAT DO WE MEAN BY CONSENT?

Let's reflect a bit about what we mean by consent. It's useful to consider consent in a more everyday context – shaking hands – and then to consider applying what we've learnt from that to sex.

THINK ABOUT IT: HANDSHAKES AND CONSENT

You can either do this activity – if there's somebody around who is up for doing it with you – or you can think through it by remembering times you've shaken hands, and imagining doing it in different ways.

1. Shake hands with someone (if you and they want to), or remember the last time you shook hands with someone. Think about how it was for you. How would you score it on a scale from 1 to 10, where 1 is terrible and 10 is amazing? *Why* did you shake their hand? *How* did you know what to do? And *what* exactly did you do (which hand, how firm, for how long, etc.)? What's the secret to a great handshake? Do you have a technique for giving a great handshake?

2. Now, try (or imagine) a handshake where you negotiate absolutely everything: checking everything out between you first. Which hand will you use? How firm will it be on a scale from 1 to 10? Do you dry your hand first? Do you shake up and down or side to side? How many shakes will there be? How long will it last? Do you want to do something else instead, like a fist bump, high five or hug? Maybe you don't want to do anything at all. Once you've finished, again ask yourself how you would

score it on a scale of 1 to 10, what it felt like for you, and how you found the process of negotiating. How did it compare to the first handshake?

3. Finally, try (or imagine) a third handshake. This time, try to experience the best of both handshakes. You're aiming to have a great handshake together, but instead of discussing it all beforehand, just check in with each other approximately what you want, then really notice everything that happens during the handshake, and use verbal or non-verbal communication to keep checking in. Look for eye contact and facial expressions: are they enjoying it? Do you nod your head, smile, laugh or make another agreeable noise? Do you ask each other how it's going or ask for things to change slightly to make it work better for you? Notice your body language: are you turning towards each other? How do your hands connect and disconnect, and how does that feel? Once you've finished, again ask yourself how you would score it on a scale from 1 to 10 and what it felt like for you. How did it compare to the other two handshakes?

You might have noticed here how similar type 1 handshakes tend to be, compared with the diversity of physical contact involved in types 2 and 3. There is a cultural script of what we're meant to do when we shake hands, and often people do the same without thinking (even if they're left-handed).

You might also have noticed how different the type 2 handshake was to the type 1. You might have been more likely to meet each other's needs, and there may have been more of a connection between you. You also knew what was going to happen. But it's also often rather awkward talking about it so much in type 2. It can feel like you lose the spontaneity, the buzz or the spark of the first handshake.

You may have found type 3 to be a bit of a balance between what was good about the type 1 and type 2 handshakes. It might also have reminded you of the 'being present' idea that we've been exploring. The idea is to really tune into yourself, the other person or people and the experience, rather than just doing something from habit, doing something 'to' another person, or – on the other hand – talking about it without actually having a sense of the experience and the ongoing process.

Handshakes are a useful analogy for sex, but they're useful as more than just an analogy too. Sex can be a very emotionally loaded area, so it can be useful to practise things like being consensual, or being present, in other areas of life in order that they become easier during sex. Think about your handshakes (or other greetings) and how you get your needs met. How does a really good handshake feel, and how does that make you feel about yourself and the other person? You might like to start bringing this up as a conversation with the people in your life and seeing how that goes.

APPLYING HANDSHAKES TO SEX!

As with type 1 handshakes, with sex mostly we default to not talking and just doing it. This kind of sex often has the same script – for example, the standard heterosexual script of kissing, undressing, 'foreplay' and PIV. As with handshakes, sometimes this kind of sex is good because it happens to work for both people. However, often it doesn't meet your needs because you haven't talked about the kind of sex you each want, and because you have the kinds of discrepancies we discussed in Chapter 4. Type 1 sex can also easily end up being non-consensual. If no-one agrees to anything, you don't check in, and 'one thing leads to another', you might think it's consensual while the other person or people do not, or vice versa. It's a bit like somebody giving us a bone-crunching handshake, thinking we'll appreciate the firmness, but we're left in pain. In this analogy, the standard one-size-fits-all kind of sex advice is a bit like the cultural script of the ideal handshake. It really isn't going to work for everyone and can easily end up being non-consensual.

The second handshake approach to sex can initially sound like a good alternative. However, in reality, many people struggle to do this when they have sex. What's good about this approach is that you've found out each other's needs beforehand and had the chance to set boundaries. Also, you have an idea of what will happen in advance, so there are less likely to be unpleasant surprises that you struggle to know what to do about in the moment. However, talking about sex in detail can be awkward, and some people feel that it kills the buzz and excitement. In a moment, we'll give you some ideas as to how you might go about having this kind of negotiation in less awkward, sexier and more fun ways. It is really important with a new person to have a good idea of what they like and their hard limits (things that would be traumatic for them). However, we might not want to have type 2 sex every time, especially with somebody we have sex with frequently.

A lot of people find that the type 3 approach works well for sex, having something of the best of both worlds of types 1 and 2. It involves really tuning into yourself and another person, and knowing that each of you really wants to do it with each other. You have enough communication to get going and are also able to check in with each other during the experience. You can also trust that you'll pay attention to whether they are enjoying it, as well as whether you are. It also emphasises non-verbal as well as verbal communication, which is how a lot of us communicate during sex. It can be good to learn about how a person likes to communicate, and what different non-verbal communication means to them, for the type 3 approach to work well.

Hopefully, you'll understand now that there's a middle way between not talking and assuming everything's consensual, and talking about everything before you do it, which will enable sex to be more consensual, more present and hopefully more enjoyable too.

WE ALL NEED TO REMEMBER: CONSENT IS IMPORTANT FOR EVERYONE, ALL THE TIME

It's so important to consider consent, whatever kinds of sex or physical contact we're having, for these key reasons:

- Most people have experienced non-consensual or unwanted sex of some kind, or sex where nobody has checked in with each other about what they like. This can be traumatising and, even when it's not, often stops people from enjoying sex.

- We frequently treat ourselves non-consensually in relation to sex: doing what we think someone else wants when we don't really want it ourselves.

- Because of the strong messages we've received about 'just doing it' and not talking openly about consent, we might well have sex that we think is consensual and then later find out that another person didn't really want it. This can leave us with a lot of guilt and shame.

- Sex generally isn't very enjoyable if we treat each other like objects that are there to give us pleasure. It generally works a lot better if we tune into ourselves and each other. However, a lot of advice suggests that people are more like machines which we just have to learn to operate properly by pressing the right buttons.

CONSENSUAL COMMUNICATION WITH YOURSELF

Now, let's look at how we might create the conditions under which good consent and communication are most possible.

One thing that people very rarely consider with consent is the idea of treating *themselves* consensually. We generally think of consent as something we have to give to – or get from – other people, not something that we could take seriously in our communication with ourselves. However, if we take our starting point as being consensual with ourselves, it may well be easier to treat other people consensually too.

We quite often treat ourselves non-consensually when it comes to sex: expecting ourselves to have sex when we don't want to, or making ourselves do things we don't want to do because we think that we should, because we're scared of losing the relationship, or because we want to appear 'normal', for example. It can be useful to think about whether we'd ever give a partner the same kind of 'you should' and 'you must' messages that we're giving ourselves, or whether we'd just go ahead and do things to them if they felt the way that we do. Can you treat yourself as well as you'd treat a friend or partner in your situation?

Treating yourself consensually is an important part of self-care (Chapter 2), and it's really useful if you can do it more broadly than just in relation to sex, as it's easier to practise sexual consent if we get used to practising consent in all areas of our lives.

It's about really knowing that it's okay to agree to or decline something, and respecting your own limits in terms of what you can and can't offer – rather than feeling that you have to go along with what other people ask of you.

For example, here is someone describing treating themselves consensually at a social event:

'I didn't want to talk with anyone because I was worried about getting pulled into a long conversation with somebody I didn't really connect with. I realised that I was treating myself non-consensually in believing that once I'd started a conversation it wasn't okay to move away. That meant I wasn't engaging with anyone at all unless I could come up with a "good excuse". I realised that an alternative would be to allow myself to honestly say when I've got to the point that I just want to be alone or with somebody I know well, rather than in a group, or to explain that I want to chat with a few different people over the course of the event.'

You can see the similarity between this and sexual situations:

'With my partner I just kind of stopped coming on to him at all because I was worried about getting pulled into a

kind of sex that wasn't really what I wanted. I realised that I was treating myself non-consensually in believing that once I'd started kissing or touching it wasn't okay to leave it at that. That meant I wasn't engaging in any kinds of physical contact at all, even though I wanted them. I realised that an alternative was to allow myself that it's fine to enjoy snogging or touching in its own right, rather than it having to lead to anything. After that happened a few times and it was okay, we ended up having sex in quite a different way to before, which worked better for me.'

Treating ourselves non-consensually can lead to us closing down because we fear the situations we might get into. For example, we might be worried that we will offer too much to somebody and have less time or energy for ourselves, that we will get into a relationship of whatever kind that doesn't feel good for us because we think that it is what the other person or people want, or that we won't feel able to change what we have to offer as we (inevitably) change over time. This can lead to an all-or-nothing approach. On the other hand, when we're consensual with ourselves we can refuse, offer only what we have to offer knowing that it is okay to change, or ask for time to consider a request or suggestion rather than responding straight away.

SEX INVENTORIES AND SEX MENUS

In order to treat yourself consensually around sex, it's useful to keep checking in with yourself to see where you're at. What turns you on currently? What are your limits? What things have changed since last time that you might want to take off – or put on – the menu?

Some people find it useful to keep a sex inventory of sexual activities and scenarios, which they can revisit over time to tune into what their current turn-ons and limits are. If you did the 'What is sex?' activity in Chapter 1, you might want to revisit that as a starting point for your list of activities and scenarios. Alternatively, you might want to start a new list now and perhaps expand your ideas about what counts as sex. The idea is to write down as many activities and scenarios that could be sexual, whether or not you like the idea of them yourself. It's worth aiming for at least 25.

Once you've got a list of everything you can think of, you can go through it saying 'yes', 'no' or 'maybe' about whether you'd like to do each one. Some people give them a rating out of 10 or add notes about how they would like to do them or with whom. It might be that some things you would enjoy exploring in fantasy but not in reality, or would only do with certain people.

This is something that you can keep for yourself or share with a partner, and you can invite them to do the same. As we already mentioned, our lists change over time, so it's worth revisiting them every year or so. Also, saying 'yes' on the list doesn't necessarily mean you'd want to do that every time, so it's still worth checking in with each other.

A sex menu is like an expanded version of a sex inventory. Here you can write in greater detail about, for example, how your body works or what kinds of scenarios really do it for you and why. You might find it useful to write a few paragraphs describing actual sexual scenarios that you find hot so that partners and potential partners can really understand how the elements come together. Or you could scrapbook in images or stories that you like. Some people like to expand it to include lists of sexy songs which capture a certain feeling that they like. Or you could do it online and include video clips. You could do it over email or messenger as more of an ongoing conversation with a partner or partners (although do be aware of the potential for other people seeing things that you share in this way). Really, it's up to you how you do it. You can find a whole zine to help you create a sex menu on our website, megjohnandjustin.com.

CONSENSUAL COMMUNICATION WITH OTHERS

What does consensual communication with other people look like if we're aiming at a 'third handshake' style approach?

The version of consent that we generally hear most about is the 'no means no' approach. This is the idea that sex is consensual so long as another person doesn't refuse our sexual invitation, or actively says 'no' (or become distressed, say 'stop' or use a safeword) during sex.

One problem with this is that research has found that people very rarely use the word 'no' when refusing things. It can, therefore, be extremely difficult to start using it in a sexual context given how unfamiliar it is. Researchers asked young people how they would tend to turn down a friend's invitation to go to the pub if they didn't want to go. Generally, they reported that they would say something like 'I'm busy,' 'I can't tonight,' or 'I've got to finish this project.' Similarly, when they were asked what they would do if they went home with somebody but then decided that they didn't want sex, people of all genders reported that they would say something like: 'I'm so sorry, I'm actually really tired,' 'I'm not sure about this,' or 'Maybe another time.'[6] So, encouraging people to actively say 'no' or listen out for a 'no' doesn't fit well with how people generally communicate.

---

[6]   Kitzinger, C. & Frith, H. (1999). Just say no? The use of conversation analysis in developing a feminist perspective on sexual refusal. *Discourse & Society*, 10(3), 293–316; O'Byrne, R., Rapley, M. & Hansen, S. (2006). 'You Couldn't Say "No", Could You?': Young Men's Understandings of Sexual Refusal. *Feminism & Psychology*, 16(2), 133–154.

THINK ABOUT IT: SAYING 'NO' AND HEARING 'NO'

Think about how easy or difficult you find it to communicate when you don't want to do something: both social things and sexual things. How do you usually communicate it? What do you do if another person doesn't realise that you're saying 'no'? Do you notice if it is easier or harder with different people, or in different situations?

How easy or difficult do you find it to hear and understand when somebody else is saying that they don't want to do something – both social things and sexual things? Do you usually feel fairly clear on this, or are you more uncertain? What do you do when you're not sure if another person is saying 'no'? Do you notice if it is easier or harder with different people, or in different situations?

This kind of finding lies behind a different idea: that we should read anything other than an active 'yes' as a 'no'. So, for example, the following kinds of things should also be read as 'no':

'I'm not sure,' 'Not now,' 'This isn't my thing,' 'I've got a partner,' 'Maybe later,' 'I'm afraid you're not my type,' 'Piss off,' 'I'd rather be alone right now,' 'Please don't touch me,' 'I really like you but …,' 'Let's just go to sleep,' 'This isn't what I want right now,' 'I've got to get up early,' 'You've been drinking,' 'I'm a bit drunk,' 'I don't feel too good,' Silence.

ACTIVE CONSENT

In the studies on how young people expressed their disinclination to do something, all the participants were clear that they would recognise statements like 'maybe' or 'I'm a bit busy' – from another person – as meaning the exact same thing as 'no'. However, there are certainly differences between people, particularly in terms of culture, class and neurodiversity, which mean that one person might struggle to read another's reluctance, especially in everyday life when they're not being asked to think carefully about these matters. For this reason, active consent can be a helpful idea. With active consent, people only go ahead if everyone involved is actively saying – or demonstrating – that they want to do so. If you're not receiving a clear, wholehearted message to go ahead from a partner, you don't go ahead, you check in with them, and they do the same with you.

As with the third handshake approach, this is an ongoing process throughout the whole encounter, rather than a one-off thing that you only do at the beginning. It's not necessarily about continually checking in verbally – 'Is this okay?' or 'Do you like this?' – although that can be good. Some kinky folks will regularly check where the other person or people are on a scale of 1 to 10, or use traffic lights to let each other know (green for go, amber for not sure, and red for stop). It might be that you each use short words or phrases to demonstrate your enjoyment, or to suggest different directions, e.g. 'This is really hot,' 'I love it when you …,' 'Down a bit,' 'A little bit softer,' 'Oh yeah, just there,' 'Please don't stop.'

Non-verbal ways of doing this include noticing how another person responds to each thing. For example, if you undo a button on their shirt, do they undo one of yours, or take their shirt off, or do they do it back up again or pull away from you? You could also tune into things like eye contact, the noises they're making, their breathing, whether they are still or moving, whether they seem more passive or more active. If they are looking away, or going very still, or their breathing or noises change in a way you're unsure about, you might well want to check in verbally to be sure.

However, as with the capacity to decline sex, the capacity to actively consent is constrained by a number of other factors, so it's important not to leave it there. There are many things that we can do in order to put in place the best possible conditions for people to engage with each other consensually.

THE WHOLE RELATIONSHIP, NOT JUST THE SEX

We can usefully ask ourselves how possible consent is in one aspect of a relationship (such as sex) if it's absent in other areas. If we find ourselves trying to force, control, pressure, persuade, cajole or manipulate our partner(s) in some areas, how easy will it be for us to adopt a different approach, or for them to be able to clearly express enthusiasm or refusal, in other areas?

This isn't easy stuff. We live in a wider society in which it is often seen as acceptable to try to gently – or not so gently – change a partner to be more like we want them to be: to nag them or niggle at them or pressure them to alter things because it would be better for us, or because we think it would be better for them. It can be easy, when we know someone well, to subtly manipulate them into doing what we want at the weekend, to pressure them into going on the kind of holiday that will make us happy, or to try to convince them to dress differently or go on a diet, for example. With new people we are dating, we can also fall into such traps – for example, if there is an expectation that one person will be the initiator in taking the other one on a date, or if we pressure somebody into drinking because it makes us feel more relaxed.

try it now MAKING YOUR WHOLE RELATIONSHIP MORE CONSENSUAL

Think about how consensual other aspects of your relationships are. You might like to open up this topic of conversation with a partner or partners and others in your life. How can you model consent when choosing a movie to watch, deciding what to have for tea, or planning a social event?

A lot of people find that if this approach becomes more of a habit in their everyday lives, it gets easier to bring it into their sex lives.

ALL RELATIONSHIPS, NOT JUST SEXUAL RELATIONSHIPS

It's difficult to cultivate the kind of consensual sexual or romantic relationships that are necessary for sex to be consensual, in large part because so few of our other relationships are consensual. Friends try to persuade each other to go to a party; parents attempt to make us try a new food; your mate pulls you up onto the dance floor; your boss disrupts you when you're trying to take a lunch break; a relative hugs and kisses you hello without checking that you're okay with it; your colleagues guilt you into going to the pub after work.

Our interpersonal relationships are shot through with non-consent on this micro level. Again, the model is often one of 'no means no' rather than of active consent. Even though we know full well that somebody's reluctance, claim to be busy, going quiet or changing the subject means that they don't want to do what we've asked, it is easy to pretend that they might still be open to it because they haven't actually said the word 'no', or to infer that they may still be up for it another time.

This kind of thing is often based on a model of scarcity rather than abundance: the assumption that there are too few people in the world for us to befriend, such that we try to make those in our lives be everything that we want or need them to be. Instead, we could recognise that there are lots of people in the world with whom we could be friends, who will each actually enjoy doing one or some of these things with us.

Some positives of a more consensual way of relating are that it can be much more enjoyable to have a coffee with somebody or an evening out when you know that the only people present are people who actively want to be there. It can also be a big relief to know that it is totally fine to reschedule or to opt out when you're feeling tired or not in the mood.

Active consent in all relationships might involve things like: asking whether somebody wants physical contact rather than assuming ('Would you like a hug?'); remembering to check in with people when there is an ongoing arrangement between you that whatever you're doing is still something that they enjoy; assuming that the lack of an enthusiastic 'yes' to an invitation means the person probably doesn't want to do what you're suggesting, and then leaving the ball in their court instead of continuing the invitations.

WE ALL NEED TO REMEMBER: DIFFERENT THINGS WORK FOR DIFFERENT PEOPLE

In any relationship, it's valuable to initiate a conversation about how you can best communicate in order that another person will feel able to decline, respecting that their way of communication might be different to yours. For example, they may find it easier to communicate about these things in writing or in person, or they could let you know that a certain response from them generally means that they are reluctant or uncomfortable.

Of course, none of this is at all easy, especially when it runs so counter to the way we've often learnt to do these things, and when we have frequently learnt to experience refusal as a personal rejection. But it's good to keep checking in with yourself about whether you're approaching people in a way that opens up, or closes down, their freedom to give consent or not (whether that's, for instance, consent to social arrangements, to work projects or to the relationship in general).

CONSENT CULTURES

When we're in wider cultures where the norm is non-consensual behaviour, it's very difficult for us to operate differently. For example, non-consensual practices are often very common in the workplace and in education. People in positions of power over others often force them to do things; implicit rules state that people should be constantly available to their colleagues; there are pressures to demonstrate 'success' in certain ways, and in competition with others.

So, we need to think about all our relationships and how cultural power dynamics play out in them. For example, do differences in age, gender, cultural background, race, body type, disability, class, family background, income, faith, role, level of sexual experiences or anything else between us mean that we have different levels of power in this situation? How do these affect the likely capacity of another person, and us, to be freely able to consent (or not) to what is being suggested? Are there pressures in play that make the other person feel that they should act enthusiastically or say 'yes', even when they're not keen? How might we bring these pressures out into the open and decrease them?

MULTIPLE EXPERIENCES: POWER DYNAMICS AND SEX

Consider these examples of the ways in which power differences between people can make consent difficult. Imagine what it might be like for the people involved.

- 'I haven't dated for quite a few years now because it's so hard to find people who don't make a thing out of my disability. When I do end up having sex with someone, I often find it hard to ask for what I want and just end up doing what they want because there's so much at stake for me.'

- 'I find it difficult to say what I want sexually because it feels like there's so much pressure on me – as a guy – to perform sex in a certain way. The medication I'm on actually makes it quite difficult to come, and it's much easier for me if I use a sex toy or my hand, rather than penetrating someone. But it feels like the expectation is so often that I should want to penetrate and to come inside somebody, and I end up trying to do that even though it isn't much fun at all.'

- 'There's so much pressure on looking a certain way in the gay scene. As a black gay man there are a lot of people who won't even consider you sexually, and then others who kind of fetishise you, which isn't great either. It makes it really hard to just have the kind of sex I want, rather than feeling the need to match up to some guy's stereotype of what a black man should be like.'

- 'I'm just always so frightened that if I don't have sex and don't come across as really into everything, he'll get bored of me and go off with somebody else. This has got worse as I've got older because it's like older bodies are automatically seen as less sexy.'

- 'I'm mindful that both my partner and I have had abusive sexual relationships in the past. In many ways that makes us very aware around consent; however, I've noticed that we can both be really cautious about suggesting anything new sexually in a way that maybe we wouldn't be if it hadn't happened.'

- 'As an asexual person, I'm really up-front that I never experience sexual attraction. I've dated a couple of people who say they're cool with that, but then it feels like they're subtly trying to coax me into sex – maybe thinking they're going to be the one who 'fixes' my asexuality. It's really offensive and hard to handle.'

- 'I've never had much money, and now I'm going out with somebody who has a lot. She always pays for dates, which is super kind, but I can't help feeling that somehow I owe her sex at the end of the evening because of it.'

Think about how your own identities, backgrounds and experiences might put you in more or less powerful positions when it comes to sex. How does this make it more or less difficult for you to consent? Which aspects widen the power gap between you and another person, what might you be able to do to narrow it? How can you maximise the potential for another person to be able to say honestly 'yes', 'no' or 'maybe' to sex with you?

NAVIGATING ONGOING RELATIONSHIPS

People often assume that consent conversations will be easier in ongoing relationships when you know somebody really well, have built up trust and have a lot of experience of physical intimacy together. However, many people find that it's actually more difficult to communicate about sex in long-term relationships because it can feel like there's a lot more at stake. For example, one research study found that people in long-term relationships only knew about 60 per cent of what their partner liked sexually, and about 20 per cent of what they didn't like,[7] which is rather terrifying if you think about it.

This is particularly hard because there are so many expectations that communicating about sex in ongoing relationships will be easy. People often assume that it's a bad sign or 'unnatural' if you actually have to talk about sex together, and that the 'right' person should telepathically know what we like and dislike. There's also a strong sense that we should stay the same over time in terms of what we like sexually, and how much we want to have sex, and any change from that – which would need communicating about – is often seen as some kind of betrayal or failure.

Communicating about sex and negotiating consent can be difficult in ongoing relationships for of a multitude of reasons, such as:

- We often become very emotionally invested in our partners finding us desirable, and it can feel scary to openly discuss something in case we end up feeling rejected by them.

- There are strong Western cultural ideas that romantic relationships should fulfil all of our needs and that we should be completely compatible with partners,

---

[7] Byers, E.S. (2005). Relationship satisfaction and sexual satisfaction: A longitudinal study of individuals in long-term relationships. *The Journal of Sex Research*, 42, 113–118.

so it can be frightening to open up any kind of conversation that might reveal discrepancies between us.

- We've come to care a great deal about this person and may be worried about hurting them by speaking about things they've done that we haven't enjoyed.

- In ongoing relationships it often means a great deal to us that our partner sees us in a positive light. This can make it extremely hard to speak up if we want something that is seen as less sexually 'normal' (e.g. having less/no sex or having kinky sex) because it would be so hard to be judged negatively by them.

- It often feels very important to regard ourselves as equal participants in an ongoing relationship, so it can become increasingly difficult to talk openly about inevitable power imbalances (e.g. differences in money, class, gender, disability, etc.) and how that impacts consent.

NEGOTIATING DISCREPANCIES

It can be extremely helpful to come to any ongoing relationship with the following assumptions:

- There will always be some discrepancies between the people involved (in terms of what they like and dislike, and how much they want to be sexual or physical).

- Everyone involved will fluctuate over time in relation to these things (over the course of a day or a week, as well as over years or decades).

Remind yourself about the diagrams of desires that you created (page 122), remembering that in any relationship there will be some areas of overlap and some areas of separation, and that these will shift over time as well.

A big part of sex communication is sharing this kind of diagram and figuring out where your areas of overlap and separation are at this particular point in time.

try it now CHECKING IN ABOUT THE OVERLAPS

In addition to drawing your desire diagrams together fairly regularly, here are a few other things you might try so as to check in with each other about where your overlaps currently are.

- Spend some time with your partner(s) reflecting on what you've recently been doing together sexually or physically: how you're each finding it, what things you're particularly enjoying, what things you might like to do more of, and anything that you would like to give a miss for a bit. Try individually to notice how into it you feel during your activities. This can tie into the idea of being present, in that you try to tune into each sensation, sound, smell or touch. Useful prompts for this kind of conversation include: 'It was hot when we …,' 'I really enjoyed it when you …,' 'I'm feeling like taking X off the menu for a while because I'm not so into it at the moment.' If you practise having these kinds of conversations, they can become more familiar and easier over time. It's important to see physical intimacy as something that happens *between* you, so it's not about blaming any one person for things that didn't work so well, but rather seeing it as an ongoing journey you're on together. Letting each other know what went well for you and complimenting each other can also be a great way of building confidence and trust.

- Make some time to share your current favourite fantasies, porn or erotic fiction. This might lead into a conversation about things you might bring into your own relationship. You might do this in online messages, or even curate an anonymous blog or bulletin app together where you save things you find particularly exciting.

- Keep an up-to-date sex menu and share this with a partner on a regular basis (e.g. once a year).

- You could go to a workshop or event together around sex and relationships where people are encouraged to do activities and discuss these kinds of things. For example, you could go to kink community events, tantra workshops or events in sex shops.

Obviously, the areas where you overlap are fairly straightforward – these are the things you're both into at the moment. However, it's still worth regularly returning to consent conversations to check in how you'll do these things consensually.

The areas of separation can be trickier to handle. It can be hard to say that there are things you used to enjoy which you'd rather not do any more, and it can be hard to hear that from another person.

If we're taking a 'third handshake' approach to sex, then hopefully we'll start to notice when we, or our partner(s), don't seem to be enjoying something as much as previously. In the moment, we might well just move on to something else, or we could check in by asking if they're enjoying this. We might also return to it afterwards: 'I was wondering whether you're still enjoying getting oral?' or 'I'm noticing I'm not feeling so into blow jobs at the moment.'

The important things here are to try to give our partner as much opportunity and encouragement as possible to be open with us, and to look after ourselves enough so that we can hear what they're saying without feeling too hurt or defensive (the self-care ideas from Chapter 2 should help with this). Also, it's important not to assume any change is once-and-for-all. Just as we may take things off the menu for a while, we may also put them back on again. If these kinds of conversations become more regular and familiar then they will feel easier over time.

If we can see sex or intimacy as something mutual (which will have some aspects that work well and others less well), then feedback will make us feel less personally vulnerable. None of this is to say that such conversations or negotiations will be pain-free. But with a foundation of self-care, the pain of acknowledging a discrepancy can become less enmeshed in a larger tangle of guilt, shame, anger or self-recrimination. Hopefully, you can stay with the feeling of loneliness that another person doesn't share what you want at the moment, or with the sadness that you can't reciprocate in the way that is desired, or with an acknowledgement of your limitations, without criticising yourself – or the other person – for it.

GETTING DESIRES MET IN AREAS OF SEPARATION

Once we have a sense of our current areas of overlap and separation, we can address the question of how we will deal with the areas of separation. Hopefully, you now have quite a range of activities you're considering here, instead of just what is culturally considered to be 'proper sex'. This is helpful because there are likely to be quite a few activities that are possible between any two or more people, as well as things that are off limits.

We've also covered the different things that we get from sexual/physical intimacy, so you'll have thought about other ways of getting those needs met which aren't sexual (see Chapter 3). This can take the pressure off a lot.

However, there are still likely to be quite a few activities in the 'separate' parts of the Venn diagram – which you don't share with any particular lover, partner or fuck-buddy. A key question then is what to do about these.

It's important to keep reminding ourselves and each other that the existence of these areas of separation is not a negative reflection on us as individuals or the relationship.

What we do about the separate activities or experiences depends on:

- How important they are to us,
- The rules of our relationship, and
- What other options are available to us.

For example, the separate areas will feel very different to us if the activities in them are something we can take or leave, and we're in an open relationship and have several partners, compared to if the activities are deeply important to us, we're in a monogamous relationship, and we don't have much access to sexual materials.

You might find it helpful to rate the activities that you don't share on a scale of 1 to 10 for how important they feel to you. You might then reflect on *why* the important ones feel so important – perhaps writing about this or talking to a friend. For example, is it important because of all the messages you've received about it being a part of 'normal' sex? Is it important because it expresses a part of yourself that you don't get to express any other way? Is it important because it's the only way in which you can reach orgasm? Revisiting the exercise you did in Chapter 3 about why you have sex might be helpful here.

Once you've unpacked which separate activities are important to you and why, you may find that there are some activities that you really want to engage with, despite it not being possible in this ongoing relationship.

RELATIONSHIP BOUNDARIES

At this point, it's vital to think about relationship boundaries. Different relationships have different boundaries in terms of what is and isn't acceptable for each person to do outside of that relationship. In long-term relationships in particular, people often find that one person stops being so interested in sex over time while the other doesn't. Thinking about our boundaries is therefore really important to ensure that a person who is more sexual gets their desires met without putting non-consensual pressure on another person.

People in different relationships will have different boundaries around sex. For example, some people may have boundaries over what they can each do (or not) with other people, what they can do alone, what they can do online or what they can do offline.

Solo sex

It's really important that each individual in a relationship is able to have solo sex of whatever kind works for them. Solo sex is a vital way of tuning into yourself, figuring out what you like, providing self-care, learning to be present and even practising self-consent. It's also a really import-ant kind of sex in its own right – no lesser than sex with other people. For these reasons, it can be very damaging to limit a person's solo sex activities.

However, because solo sex *is* a form of sex, it's under-standable that some people struggle to know that their partner(s) are enjoying sex on their own. If you find it dif-ficult when someone you're having sex with has solo sex, it's worth remembering that solo sex is an option to you too. It may well help you each to enjoy partner sex more, and it can take the pressure off partner sex if you have dif-ferent levels or types of desire. There's also the possibility of enjoying fantasies, stories, images or videos in solo sex of a kind that your partner(s) don't enjoy, and vice versa.

Of course, there are some situations in which one person's solo sex does feel difficult for their partner(s) – for example, if they have so much solo sex that they disengage from the other person or people, or if they're doing something in solo sex that feels unethical or non-consensual to their partner(s). In these situations, as with all relationship conflicts, it's worth talking about it (either together or with a relationship therapist if it becomes really difficult).

It's worth thinking about how you negotiate solo sex, particularly if you share living space some or all of the time. As with other kinds of sex, such conversations could usefully cover:

- *What does and doesn't feel okay to each person concerned:* Any limits, such as maybe you're not comfortable with them doing it in bed next to you if you're not feeling horny yourself; perhaps it's important for you to have the freedom to do it once a day, including when you're on holiday together; maybe you'd prefer it if they clear up the sex toys afterwards.

- *How much each person wants to know:* For example, 'Don't ask don't tell,' 'Let me know when you're having solo sex so I can give you some privacy,' 'I'd love to hear the details because it turns me on.'

- *How you'll let each other know that you want some solo sex:* Some people will just say it directly, others have code words, like: 'You go to the pub, I'm going to have a quiet night in,' 'I'll be back in a tick, just going to re-grout the bathroom,' 'Ooh I had a good hard think earlier today.' You might also think about how you're going to communicate whether you're feeling horny and would happily do something together, or separately if your partner isn't in the mood, or whether it's particularly solo sex that you're in the mood for. This can be similar, of course, to negotiating when you're going to watch TV, do some chores or have a meal together or separately.

Sex with more than one person

People have a wide range of different boundaries around sex with other people in their relationships. This is something that has been talked about much more openly in the last couple of decades, and a lot of language has developed for different forms of monogamy and non-monogamy that are open – to different extents – to people having multiple sexual partners. For example, monogamish relationships are somewhat open; soft swingers do some physical contact with other people but not others; solo-polys are independent people who may have several sexual partners; people in open relationships have sex partners beyond their primary couple.

THINK ABOUT IT: SEX BOUNDARIES

Where are your boundaries, for yourself and your partners, around having sex with other people? You might find it useful to imagine this on the spectrum from Chapter 4. At one end are people who have no kind of physical or flirty contact with anybody other than their partner. At the other end are people who can be sexual with anybody they feel like with no rules or agreements. In between, you might think about people who agree that it's okay to flirt with other people, to have cybersex, to do certain physical acts but not sex, to have sex but only with strangers or sex workers, or to have sex but only if they are present (e.g. threesomes). You could think about which boundaries are preferences and which are absolutely necessary for you, and why. You could also think about whether it's easier to express boundaries that are common in wider culture compared to those which aren't.

Once you've thought about where your boundaries are, you might also find it helpful to think about where your boundaries have been in the past, whether this has changed over time, and where you imagine them being in the future. You can also think about where you imagine your current (or past) partner's or partners' boundaries are, and whether you're in the same place or different places. Hopefully, this can lead into a useful discussion.

Many people find that even if they're using the same words to describe their relationship (e.g. monogamous or polyamorous) what they *mean* by this can be somewhat different. For example, some people's monogamy is open to porn and some isn't, some people's poly includes still being each other's 'most important person' and some people's doesn't.

The important point is that wherever somebody is on this spectrum is fine: there's no right or wrong place to be. However, of course it can be tricky if two or more partners are in different places. If so, you might think about whether either or both of you might feel okay moving your position on the spectrum, whether a compromise is possible, whether you can agree to differ, or whether it does require a greater change in your relationship. It's also worth talking about whether you want to make a clear agreement in your relationship or keep it more flexible and open, and how much you want to let each other know about other physical/sexual relationships. Similar conversations are also helpful around the levels of emotional closeness that you have with other people.

SEX COMMUNICATION AS SEX

Throughout this chapter, we've been trying to remove the distinction between sex communication and sex itself: changing that idea that sex communication is something we might do before we have sex to ensure consent, or after we have sex to debrief. As the third handshake approach suggests, it's great if we can question this distinction between communicating and sex.

It's great for enjoying sex, and for consent, if we see communication as something that happens throughout sex, and if we view our sex communication as a kind of sex in its own right. Here are some examples of how this can work before, during and after sex.

MULTIPLE EXPERIENCES: COMMUNICATION AS PART OF SEX

- *Before:* 'My last relationship started over messenger. We lived at a distance, so it was a while before we could make an in-person date. As we got to know each other, we started sharing our sexual interests over messenger. This was very hot, and we even wound up having sex a couple of times that way (describing what we were doing to each other) before we had sex in person. It definitely took the pressure off the first time we had in-person sex.'

- *Before:* 'On the train journey over to see my partner, she would ask me what I wanted: everything from what she was wearing to what we wanted to do the moment I got through the door. We texted each other for twenty minutes like this, which was really hot, so by the time the door opened we were both really up for it. Even if we didn't end up doing the things we'd talked about doing, we both enjoyed that build-up.'

- *During:* 'My partner often talks to me during sex, describing things that he's imagining doing to me, which might not be what we're actually doing. For example, anal sex is quite difficult for us because of our body shapes, but he'll often talk like that's what he's doing, which is totally horny. Also, I don't have a cock but like being talked to as if I do, while he's touching me.'

- *During:* 'Once I started really paying attention to the noises that my partner and I make during sex, I started to enjoy sex a lot more. When we both do this, we get this amazing sense of a building excitement during sex as we breathe and moan increasingly heavily and loudly. Knowing that we're both really into it gives us a positive feedback loop, making sex super-hot for both of us.'

- *After:* 'For me, kinky sex is often all about aftercare. Really, the whole point of the scene is to get my partner to a certain psychological state. We do negotiate the scene beforehand, and I also talk to them during to check in how they're doing and how much more they can take. But what we're both really looking for is for me to push them to their edge so that they can let go, often crying with the release of physical sensation and submission. Then it's all about my nurturing them, looking after them, telling them how good they've been and how wonderful they are.'

- *After:* 'Me and my two partners often do a kind of post-match analysis after we've had sex together. It often starts just with listening to each other's noises! Like contented sighs all round, or sometimes we all end up giggling together. Then someone will say something like "That was great" or "Pass me the tissues," and we'll just start talking about what we enjoyed, or checking in how some new element was for each of us. It's always okay to say whatever we feel in that space. Sometimes we've tried something that doesn't work at all, and that's just as okay as something being brilliant.'

Where Do We Go from Here?

You've reached the end of the book! We've covered a lot of material in the last five chapters. Some of it you might have found challenging. Some of it will definitely have been pretty different to what you have heard before. We do hope that you've found it useful, but it's worth being mindful that you're unlikely to put everything we've covered into practice right away. It certainly takes a long time to let go of some of the crappy messages that we've all received about sex.

Enjoying sex is a lifelong process, and you may well find yourself coming back to the ideas here at different times. That's certainly our experience. Every time we think about one of these topics – solo sex or consent, for example – we find we sink a little deeper with it and see something we hadn't quite seen before. Even writing this book, we both found ourselves learning things and applying them to our lives in ways we hadn't quite managed before.

try it now ENJOYABLE AND NOT ENJOYABLE SEX

To continue this journey, you might well find it useful to return to the first exercise in Chapter 1 about enjoying sex: comparing enjoyable times to less enjoyable ones. It will be interesting to reflect on what has changed since you started the book. You might find it helpful to keep coming back to this same activity over the years as a way of checking where you're at with sex.

So, you need to think of an erotic, sexual or sensual experience that you've had – one time when you enjoyed it and another time when it was less enjoyable. Try to remember both experiences in rich detail: writing a description or just thinking it through.

For each experience – the enjoyable one, and the not-so-enjoyable one – in turn think about:

- *How it started:* Where were you? What was happening beforehand? How did it begin? How did you feel? What sensations were involved? What thoughts were going through your head?

- *How it progressed:* What happened next? What were your feelings, sensations and thoughts? Run through the time in your head, continuing to tune into the feelings, sensations and thoughts.

- *How it ended:* What was that like? How did you feel afterwards?

Now think about any differences that you notice between the two times, and reflect on how your answers might have changed since you first did this activity.

The more that you can tune into what is, and isn't, working for you – rather than what you think you should do and what should work – the better you'll be able to enjoy sex.

We've now given you the tools that you need to be your own 'sexpert'. There is no one-size-fits-all set of answers, but hopefully now you have what you need to keep learning how you enjoy sex, and to approach anybody else in the same way.

There are many links between how we approach sex and how we approach the rest of our lives. Learning self-care and being present, tuning into our bodies, and communicating openly and consensually with others are all really helpful in life in general, not just in our sex lives. The more we learn these things in sex, the more we can apply them to the rest of our lives, and vice versa. We hope you too will find that many of the ideas and practices you've learnt in this book will be helpful to you way beyond the sexual parts of your life.

Further Resources

Throughout this book, we've been pretty critical about mainstream sex advice. However, there are some great sex advice resources available, in addition to all of those that we find questionable! Here's a list of some of the resources you might find helpful if you want to explore the topics in each chapter of the book further.

We've also produced our own zines to give you more of a structured way in which to think through your own sexual desires and relationship preferences. You can find those and a whole load more resources, blog posts and problem-page answers on our website at megjohnand justin.com.

Preface

If you're feeling unsure about your relationship, these websites are helpful:

- 'Blinders off: Getting a good look at abuse and assault' by Heather Corinna, scarleteen.com

- 'Signs of an abusive relationship' by Justin Hancock, bishuk.com.bishuk.com/relationships/abusive -relationships-2/

- 'Worried that your partner is emotionally abusive?' by Emma Rust, everydayfeminism.com

If you think your relationship might be unsafe or abusive, please check out Mind's list of support organisations for people dealing with abuse, assault or rape:

mind.org.uk/information-support/
guides-to-support-and-services/abuse/sexual-abuse

Chapter 1: Introduction

Some great sex advice that we rate highly happens on the following websites. Of course, different kinds of advice suit different people so it's worth checking them out and seeing which appeal most to you.

- Cory Silverberg's 'About Sexuality', sexuality.about.com

- Paul Joannides's 'Guide to Getting It On', guidetogettingiton.com

- Dr Petra Boynton's advice column at the *Daily Telegraph*, telegraph.co.uk/journalists/petra-boynton

- Tania Glyde's blog, 'London Central Counselling' – for example, this piece 'Are you stuck on the Sex Escalator?', londoncentralcounselling.com/2016/04/05/are-you -stuck-on-the-sex-escalator

- Dan Savage's 'Savage Love' column and podcast, savagelovecast.com

- Jo Adams's book provides a holistic approach to sex and relationships education: *Explore, Dream, Discover: Working with holistic models of sexual health and sexuality, self-esteem and mental health*. (2004). Sheffield: Centre for HIV and Sexual Health.

- Emily Nagoski's website – emilynagoski.com – and books, including her titles in the 'Good in Bed' series and *Come as You Are: The surprising new science that will transform your sex life*. (2015). New York, London: Simon & Schuster.

- For younger folk, we would recommend scarleteen.com and Justin's own site bishuk.com

Some of the questions we've raised in this book come out of a more academic project that Meg-John was involved with. If you're interested in reading more it's covered in this book:

- Barker, M.J., Gill, R. & Harvey, L. (forthcoming, 2017). *Mediated Intimacy: Sex advice in media culture.* London: Polity.

Chapter 2: You and Sex
Here are some good resources about being present and mindfulness. It's worth looking at the blurb for each one and seeing which one seems to suit you best.

- Meg-John's 'Staying With Feelings' zine – available from rewriting-the-rules.com

- Batchelor, M. (2001). *Meditation for Life*. London: Frances Lincoln.

- Chödrön, P. (2001). *The Wisdom of No Escape: How to love yourself and your world*. London: HarperCollins.

- Parks, T. (2010). *Teach Us to Sit Still: A sceptic's search for health and healing*. London: Vintage.

- Williams, J.M. & Penman, D. (2011). *Mindfulness: A practical guide to finding peace in a frantic world*. London: Piatkus.

Some useful resources which cover sexual fantasies, erotica and solo sex include:

- Barker, M.J. (forthcoming, 2017). *Psychology of Sex*. London: Routledge and Psychology Press.
- Morin, J. (2012). *The Erotic Mind: Unlocking the inner sources of passion and fulfillment*. London: HarperCollins.
- Dubberley, E. (2013). *Garden of Desires: The evolution of women's sexual fantasies*. London: Black Lace.
- Girl on the Net's blog, girlonthenet.com, and two books: *Girl on the Net: How a bad girl fell in love*. (2016). London: Blink Publishing; *My Not-So-Shameful Sex Secrets*. (2016). CreateSpace.

This is a great book aimed particularly at younger women:

- Friedman, J. (2011). *What You Really Really Want: The smart girl's shame-free guide to sex and safety*. Berkeley, CA: Seal Press.

Chapter 3: Bodies
Some good books about diverse bodies include:

- Jenkins, E. (1999). *Tongue First: Adventures in physical culture*. New York, Virago.
- Cooke, K. (1996). *Real Gorgeous: The truth about body and beauty*. London: Bloomsbury.

If you want to learn more about the anatomy of the body, including genitals, then Cyndi Darnell's 'Atlas of Erotic Arousal' resources are really helpful:

- cyndidarnell.com/atlas-of-erotic-anatomy-arousal.

For more on disability in particular, this book is great:

- Kaufman, M., Silverberg, C. & Odette, F. (2003). *The Ultimate Guide to Sex and Disability: For all of us who live with disabilities, chronic pain or illness*. San Francisco, CA: Cleis Press.

Outsiders provides support for people with disabilities around bodies, sex, relationships and dating:

- outsiders.org.uk

A couple of useful books on specific sexual practices are:

- Carellas, B. (2007). *Urban Tantra: Sacred sex for the twenty-first century*. Berkeley, CA: Celestial Arts.
- Taormino, T. (Ed.) (2012). *The Ultimate Guide to Kink: BDSM, role play and the erotic edge*. Berkeley, CA: Cleis Press.

Chapter 4: Relationships

Some books and websites which cover the diversity of ways of doing relationships:

- Perel, E. (2007). *Mating in Captivity: Sex, lies and domestic bliss*. London: HarperCollins.

- Taormino, T. (2008). *Opening Up: A guide to creating and sustaining open relationships*. Berkeley, CA: Cleis Press.

- Franklin Veaux's polyamory site, morethantwo.com, and book of the same name, co-authored with Eve Rickert, *More than Two*. (2014). Portland, OR: Thorntree Press.

- 'Solo poly: Life, relationships and dating as a free agent', solopoly.net and offescalator.com

- Andie Nordgren's resources on relationship anarchy, relationship-anarchy.com/blog

Good books and websites on how to manage relationships are:

- Barker, M. (2013). *Rewriting the Rules: An integrative guide to love, sex and relationships*. London: Routledge.

- Barker, M.J. & Gabb, J. (2016). *The Secrets of Enduring Love: How to Make Relationships Last*. London: Penguin RandomHouse.

- Lerner, H. (2003). *The Dance of Intimacy: A woman's guide to courageous acts of change in key relationships*. New York: William Morrow Paperbacks.

- Lerner, H. (2001). *The Dance of Connection: How to talk to someone when you're mad, hurt, scared, frustrated, insulted, betrayed, or desperate*. New York: HarperCollins.

- Welwood, J. (2006). *Perfect Love, Imperfect Relationships: Healing the wound of the heart*. Boston, MA: Trumpeter.

- S. Bear Bergman's 'Ask Bear' problem page, the-toast .net/series/ask-bear

For more on asexuality specifically, see:

- Sam Broadley's documentary 'Taking the Cake' (2015). https://youtu.be/AkboMcOSmBc
- The AVEN (Asexual Visibility and Education Network) website, asexuality.org

Chapter 5: Communication and Consent

In addition to the resources on managing relationships mentioned for Chapter 4, some further good resources on consent and communication include:

- Betty Martin's 'Wheel of Consent', bettymartin.org/ videos
- Meredith Reynolds' 'Playing Well With Others' series of blog posts: meredith-reynolds.com/blog

The following websites introduce how to write your own sex menu or relationship user manual:

- Our website, megjohnandjustin.com
- The Sex Menu Site, sexmenus.wordpress.com
- Polyamory Weekly's user manual, polyweekly.com/tag/ user-manual

For support services for people dealing with abuse, assault or rape, Mind provides a long list of helpful services:

- mind.org.uk/information-support/guides-to-support -and-services/abuse/sexual-abuse

Index